ATTACK OF
THE COPULA SPIDERS

ATTACK
OF THE
COPULA
SPIDERS

and
OTHER
ESSAYS ON
WRITING

DOUGLAS GLOVER

BIBLIOASIS

Library and Archives Canada Cataloguing in Publication

Glover, Douglas, 1948–
    Attack of the copula spiders : and other essays on writing / Douglas Glover.

ISBN 978-1-926845-46-3

    1. Authorship.   I. Title.

PS8563.L64A87 2012   c814'.54   c2011-907872-4

Canada Council   Conseil des Arts
for the Arts   du Canada

ONTARIO ARTS COUNCIL
CONSEIL DES ARTS DE L'ONTARIO

Canadian   Patrimoine
Heritage   canadien

Biblioasis acknowledges the ongoing financial support of the Government of Canada through The Canada Council for the Arts, Canadian Heritage, the Canada Book Fund; and the Government of Ontario through the Ontario Arts Council.

For Melissa

CONTENTS

HOW TO
WRITE A NOVEL

THE FOLLOWING is a synopsis of a lecture I have given
dozens of times on how to put a novel together. I always
deliver the lecture extemporaneously. It is never the
same twice. And when I have tried to write it out, it goes dead at
my fingertips. I've come to think of it as oral lore, not meant
to be fixed on the page. But I have, over the years, managed to
write a short summary of the lecture to send out to students
when they need their memories refreshed. The disadvantage
of this summary is that it is too concise and didactic, a bit of
a sketch. It reads like a prescription: take two of these, and a
novel will pop out of you in a week. I wish it were that easy. The
advantage of it is that I deal with structures the craft books and
the literary critics never tell aspiring writers about. How to construct a point of view. How to construct a subplot. How to think
up a theme. How to construct an image pattern. How characters
in a novel think. How all these elements relate to one another.

In any case, readers should try to ignore the prescriptive
language and imagine, first of all, that I am telling them how to
read a novel. Then they should go to a novel they love and try
to read it for the structures I have suggested are basic to the

writing of novels. The beauty of form is its infinite variability. Experimental novels tend to take some of the structures I talk about and invert them or emphasize them differently than a conventional novel. But the structures remain roughly the same. Some novelists use very little image patterning. Sometimes the subplot gets confined to an amazingly tiny amount of text. Sometimes backfill expands to form a plot parallel to the main plot. Occasionally, an author will invent a device that does the job of, say, a subplot but isn't exactly a subplot. Tim O'Brien does this in his novel *In the Lake of the Woods*, where, instead of a subplot, he writes multiple speculative versions of the main plot. Obviously, my model is based on a simplest-case scenario: single character first- or third-person narrative. But the reader won't have to think too hard to figure out how what I say about point of view plays in a third-person multiple narrative or a first-person reminiscent narrative.

I break down the novel into six major structures: point of view, plot, novel thought, subplot, theme and image patterning. In any actual novel, these structures are intricately folded together to form an organic unity. Teasing them apart for the purpose of discussing them separately in this present context creates an artificial impression of distinctness. Also it is important to realize that a novel is an illusion. A narrative seems to flow through time when, in fact, it is made up of a number of static structures: scenes, events, event sequences, reflective devices, repetitions, all of which are nothing but words fixed on the page. The first time we read a novel we read to experience the flow of time; it is only on rereading the book over and over that we begin to see the static structures that give the illusion of life.

Point of View

Point of view is the mental modus operandi of the person who is telling or experiencing the story—most often this is the protagonist. This mental modus operandi is located in a fairly simple construct involving desire, significant history and language overlay. The writer generally tries to announce the desire, goal or need of the primary character as quickly as possible. The key here is to make this desire concrete and simple. In *Anna Karenina*, Anna wants to be with Vronsky. In Joyce Cary's *The Horse's Mouth*, Gulley Jimson wants to paint pictures. In Kingsley Amis's *Lucky Jim*, Jim wants to keep his teaching job. Concrete simplicity at the outset can yield to generalization down the line if only because, with a thematic sentence here and there, any particular desire can be tweaked into standing for all human striving and aspiration. The important thing to remember: the novel is a machine of desire.

Significant history is background material that tells the story of how the main character arrives at the beginning of the novel wanting what he wants. Its significance derives from its relationship to the character's concrete desire and current situation. History that does not relate directly to this desire is superfluous. It often makes the narrative turn flabby or worse—boring (the reader yawns, loses concentration). The important thing to remember is that significant history can be kept brief but needs to be repeated (via references, expansions, variations). These repetitions begin to give the novel a rhythm and a memory. Unless you have a really good reason for not doing so, make sure that the character is passionately engaged with his desire and current situation. Don't give someone, say, a job that doesn't mean anything—a job, social station and life circumstances should connect up with desire in a significant way. Keep things passionate (love, obviously, but don't forget the negative passions—hatred and anger and fear). Once you have the desire and significant history in place, then you'll have a fairly clear idea how your character will react as new situations arise—hence the modus operandi idea.

The device of language overlay involves diction, syntax and figurative language: your character needs to talk and think in terms that reflect his passionate attachment to life (desire and significant history). For example, in my novel *Precious* the protagonist is a newspaperman; on the first page of the novel, a tavern hides across a street "like an overlooked misprint between jutting office towers." At another point, the protagonist starts thinking in newspaper headlines. Conversely, it would have been a faux pas to have him start thinking in sailing metaphors. Here is Gulley Jimson, a passionate painter, describing the Thames in *The Horse's Mouth*: "Sun all in a blaze. Lost its shape. Tide pouring up from London as bright as bottled ale. Full of bubbles and every bubble flashing its own electric torch. Mist breaking into round fat shapes, china white on Dresden blue. Dutch angels by Rubens della Robbia. Big one on top curled up with her knees to her nose like the little marble woman Dobson did for Courtauld. A beauty." The diction and figurative language are drawn straight from the heart of the perceiving subject.

Plot

Plot is rather complicated and to discuss it we need to break it down into smaller issues. I like to draw what I call railroad track diagrams (an exercise that can be tried at any point in the writing process—at the beginning or after several drafts). By railroad track diagrams I mean train tracks as they are often represented on maps: a single line with perpendicular crossbars at regular intervals. If you draw this as a semi-circular arch, it brings to mind an "arc of action." Later, as you develop scenes, events, sequences of events, and/or plot steps you can attach little balloons with text to the perpendicular crossbars and the train track becomes a plot diagram. But start by putting an A at one end and a B at the other. A needs to be a question. Generally this question relates to the concrete desire of the protagonist: will he get what he wants? It's very simple. The end of the novel then becomes equally simple. B will be an answer to the question: yes or no. Answering yes or no doesn't limit you as to tone or degree of closure. You can immediately add a structural but-construction to shade this simple answer. For example, Bill wants to marry Sue, Bill gets to marry Sue, but he discovers that he is gay and locked in a loveless marriage. In *Lucky Jim*, Jim wants to keep his job teaching at a third-rate English university. By the end of the novel, he has lost his job but found a much better one. In *Anna Karenina*, Anna wants to be with Vronsky. By the end of the novel, she has gotten her wish, but the reality of life with Vronsky drives her to despair and suicide. In *The Horse's Mouth*, Gulley finally gets to paint his masterpiece, but the wall he is painting it on is demolished and he ends up in hospital. But—this is a double but ending—he is happy. In any case, deciding how the question will be answered gives you the general direction of the book.

Next you begin to fill in between A and B with events, plot steps or scenes. (In a novel, scenes don't always correspond to plot steps—at least to my way of thinking. An event or a plot step might involve a sequence of scenes and summary. I tend to use terms like "plot step" or "event" or "event sequence" so that students don't jump straight to the idea of "scene." Part of this is a question of level as well. At a certain level, a novel plot might consist of six large actions—call them events or event sequences or plot steps, but each of these might be broken down into a number of smaller events, sequences of events, plot steps, or scenes, and so on.) Sometimes you have a few events in your head or a collection of characters and an ending. Sometimes you already have a whole novel draft to work with. In any case, you now begin to fill in those little balloons attached to the railroad tracks in the diagram with notes about events. You try to put them in order, arrange a rough sequence and a climax. Then you keep doing versions of this as you add more events and as you reconstruct events based on certain other structural principles that need to be taken into consideration.

For example, you need to think of the novel as a dramatic action: intention (desire, question)-resistance (conflict)-climax. The key here is to develop a consistent resistance, the force pushing against the achievement of the concrete desire. The novel as a whole will have a dramatic structure, but each event along the way to the climax needs also to have a dramatic structure which is a smaller version of the larger dramatic structure. The main character will go into each scene or event or plot step wanting something, usually something that will help him attain that concrete goal, and then he encounters resistance. You can think of every scene or event as a win-lose situation and you decide (and this is a decision of tone—light or dark—and a decision of structure—will the character ultimately achieve his goal?) how close or how far from winning the character comes in each scene.

Then, finally, you need to construct your sequence of events and scenes so that each leads logically into the next. I say "logically" where a lot of how-to writers say "causally"—both words evade the essential issue. In each scene, you have a situation and a conflict and a win or loss at the end; and at the end of each scene you need to get into the shoes of your primary character and "feel" what he wants to do next. The key here is to realize that what I call "ordinary human motivation" is the causal factor moving the plot from one event to another. Just keep asking yourself: given what's happened and what my character wants, what does he do next (this can be as simple as deciding where he points his feet when he takes his next step)? You then need to test your sequence of events on this what-would-he-do-next? line.

This should give you a fairly solid plot—and, of course, you'll probably be writing the novel as you produce these successive train track models. It's important to realize that this kind of experiment with scene and sequence is not exactly an outline. Rather it's a process of thinking about plot. It's not the sort of thing one does once and never has to return to again. It's an evolving project. In every novel I have written, I have found sequences that needed to be re-plotted again and again, either taking out or putting in steps. This is partly because writing is driven by sentences; sentences you write at the beginning of a novel can have drastic effects, even at the level of plot, as the novel develops.

Novel Thought

In connection with plot, creating plot and plot continuity, novelists use what I call novel thought to sew the novel together. Novel thought is very stylized and systematic, unlike real thought. It functions by concentrating on time and motive. Characters are always doing three things:

1) Looking back, remembering where they have been and why they have come to where they are. This happens over and over, obsessively, as it were, so that the reader is forever being reminded of the character's past or earlier events in the novel as seen from the character's perspective as well as the character's current motivation. For example, here is Gulley Jimson in *The Horse's Mouth* thinking at the end of a scene in which he has telephoned his old patron Hickson and tried to extract more money from him, this after just being released from jail for harassing the same man. Gulley suffers from what we now call poor impulse control.

> In fact, I realized that I had been getting upset. I hadn't meant to say anything about burning Hickson's house down. Now, when I say anything like that, about shooting a man or cutting his tripes out, even in a joke, I often get angry with him. And anything like bad temper is bad for me. It spoils my equanimity. It blocks up my imagination.

It makes me stupid so that I can't see straight. But luck-
ily I noticed it in time. Cool off, I said to myself. Don't get
rattled off your centre. Remember that Hickson is an old
man. He's nervous and tired of worry. That's his trouble,
worry. Poor old chap, it's ruining any happiness he's got
left. He simply don't know what to do. He sends you to
jug and it makes him miserable, and as soon as you come
out you start on him again. And he's afraid that if he gives
you any money, you'll come after him more than ever and
fairly worry him to death.

2) Assessing where they are now: What am I doing? Why am I
doing it? Why is that other character doing what he is doing?
What does this look like? What does it remind me of? (Thought
is action. Characters don't necessarily have to be right in their
assessments, they just have to be true to themselves in the context of what's gone before.) Here is Jim Dixon thinking in *Lucky
Jim*. He's at a dance party with a set of awful phonies, but he is
hoping to meet up with a girl who turns out to be his major love
interest. He steps outside to wait. Note the run of rhetorical
questions, a classic device of novel thought.

Feeling less hot, Dixon heard the band break into a tune
he knew and liked; he had the notion that the tune was
going to help out this scene and fix it permanently in his
memory; he felt romantically excited. But he'd got no
business to feel that, had he? What was he doing here,
after all? Where was it all going to lead? Whatever it was
leading towards, it was certainly leading away from the
course his life had been pursuing for the last eight months,
and this thought justified his excitement and filled him
with reassurance and hope. All positive change was good;
standing still, growing to the spot, was always bad. He
remembered somebody once showing him a poem which

ended something like "Accepting dearth, the shadow of death." That was right, not "experiencing dearth," which happened to everybody. The one indispensable answer to an environment bristling with people and things one thought were bad was to go on finding out new ways in which one could think they were bad. The reason why Prometheus couldn't get away from his vulture was that he was keen on it, and not the other way around.

3) Looking ahead: Given what's just happened, what do I want to do next? What plan can I make? What do I think the other character(s) will do next? How will I react to that? Here is Jim Dixon again, planning for a lecture on which his academic career depends.

Avoiding thinking about Margaret, and for some reason not wanting to think about Christine, he found his thoughts turning toward his lecture. Early the previous evening he'd tried working his notes for it up into a script. The first page of notes had yielded a page and three lines of script. At that rate he'd be able to talk for eleven and a half minutes as his notes now stood. Some sort of pabulum for a further forty-eight and a half minutes was evidently required, with perhaps another minute off for being introduced to the audience, another minute for water-drinking, coughing, and page-turning, and nothing for applause or curtain calls. Where was he going to find this supplementary pabulum? The only answer to this question seemed to be . . . Yes, that's right, where? Ah, wait a minute; he'd get Barclay to find him a book on medieval music. Twenty minutes at least on that, with an apology for "having let my interest run away with me." Welch would absolutely eat that. He blew bubbles for a moment with the milk in his spoon at the thought of having to transcribe so many hateful facts, then cheered up at the thought of being able to do himself so much good without having to think at all. "It may perhaps be thought," he muttered to himself, "that the character of an age, a nation, a class, would be but poorly revealed in anything so apparently divorced from ordinary habits of thought as its music, as its musical culture." He leant forward impressively over the cruet. "Nothing could be further from the truth."

These various kinds of thought, their temporal modes (call them recapitulative, grounding and anticipatory), should be in the text continuously. Characters should always be connecting events in their own heads (so the reader can remember and see the connection). Every chapter, event, plot step or scene should have some memory of or reference to earlier events (that is, every movement forward in the text needs to include a glance back). And every chapter, event, plot step or scene should look ahead, that is, have reference to what's coming up (in the form of a plan or an expression of desire or fear, etc.). All these references occur in the point-of-view character's mind, in novel thought.

Over and over in novels you'll find a pattern. The chapter opens, then there will be a tiny bit of backfill connecting this chapter to the last one, maybe a summary of events or plot steps leading to this point, and a clear sense of what the character plans to get out of the coming scene(s). Then, as the chapter closes, you will find a section of reflection on what has just happened and a moment of decision or planning—Where do I turn next? A novel is always making connections with itself in the form of novel thought; novel thought links events by reminding the reader of what's already happened in the text, and, crucially, by establishing motivation for what's to come. (A corollary of this principle is that if you can't write a piece of novel thought that logically connects one event with the next, then you almost certainly have a plot problem.)

Finally, it's important to see how novel thought connects with the device of point of view, the narrating consciousness of the novel, or the modus operandi of this narrating consciousness. I talked earlier about point of view in terms of concrete desire, significant history and language overlay. Now add to this the idea that novel thought must be an expression of the point of view complex. It's important for any novelist to invent a point of view that can perceive the world of the novel adequately. By "adequately," I mean the point of view needs to be able to filter for the reader all the facets, complications, interrelationships, histories, ironies and nuances the novelist wishes to get across. Many beginning novelists mistakenly limit themselves by faulty invention of point of view, that is, they invent a point of view too stupid or inarticulate or psychologically limited to see the world of the novel properly. Here is Henry James, in his preface to *The Golden Bowl*, writing about his point of view structure:

> The Prince, in the first half of the book, virtually sees and knows and makes out, virtually represents to himself everything that concerns us . . . Having a consciousness highly susceptible of registration, he thus makes us see the things that may most interest us reflected in it . . . and yet after all never a whit to the prejudice of his being just as consistently a foredoomed, entangled, embarrassed agent in the general imbroglio, actor in the given play. The function of the Princess, in the remainder, matches exactly with his; the register of her consciousness is as closely kept—as closely, say, not only as his own, but as that (to cite examples) either of the intelligent but quite unindividualised witness of the destruction of "The Aspern Papers," or of the all-noting heroine of "The Spoils of

Poynton," highly individualised though highly intelligent; the Princess, in fine, in addition to feeling everything she has to, and to playing her part just in that proportion, duplicates, as it were, her value and becomes a compositional resource, and of the finest order, as well as a value intrinsic.

Subplot

You need to have a clear idea of your plot structure in order to construct an appropriate subplot. A subplot or subplot-like device is a distinguishing characteristic of the novel as opposed to the short story; you need at least one for a novel (of course, there are exceptions, but they are usually very short novels), whereas in short stories you can do without them. In its simplest and most direct form the subplot is another plot, involving another set of characters, weaving through the novel (obviously, characters can and do act on both plot and subplot lines). Sometimes a subplot expands to about the same amount of text as the main plot and becomes a parallel plot.

As I say, you have to know how the main plot works in order to construct the subplot because the subplot has to bear a particular relationship to the main plot: it has to be congruent or antithetical. In *Anna Karenina*, for example, the plot is about Anna's adulterous and tragic affair with Vronsky. The subplot, bulked up in terms of the amount of text to a parallel plot, is about Levin's dutiful and successful marriage. The plot and subplot are opposites (and there is a third plot—the Oblonsky plot, also a story of adultery—which is congruent with the main plot). I know I make this sound a bit geometrical. Aldous Huxley in *Point Counter Point* has his novel-writing character describe it slightly differently: "A novelist modulates by reduplicating situations and characters. He shows several people falling in love, or dying, or praying in different ways—dissimilars solving the same problem. Or, *vice versa*, similar people confronted with dissimilar problems."

If the subplot bears the proper relation to the main plot, then you get the resonating or echoing effect that you want. To my mind, this subplot resonance is the key to what we call the "aliveness" of a novel—contrary to popular opinion, which seems to hold that aliveness comes from verisimilitude. Subplot resonance is also one of the ways of giving a novel the sense of being about a world teeming with people, when it will most often be about a small group of characters. In a little essay on *King Lear*, W. B. Yeats called the effect of subplotting "the emotion of multitude."

> The Shakespearian drama gets the emotion of multitude out of the subplot which copies the main plot, much as a shadow upon the wall copies one's body in the firelight . . . Lear's shadow is in Gloucester, who also has ungrateful children, and the mind goes on imagining shadows, shadow beyond shadow, till it has pictured the world. In *Hamlet*, one hardly notices, so subtly is the web woven, that the murder of Hamlet's father and the sorrow of Hamlet are shadowed in the lives of Fortinbras and Ophelia and Laertes, whose fathers, too, have been killed.

Generally, subplots involve a second or third set of characters who are closely related to the main set of characters. Tolstoy, in his letters, said he always used other family members as subplot characters. In *Anna Karenina*, the main plot is between Anna and Vronsky, the parallel plot is between Levin and Kitty, and the smaller subplot is between Oblonsky (Anna's brother) and his wife (Kitty's sister). Anne Tyler also uses family members for subplot characters in her novel *The Accidental Tourist* (main plot—Macon and the dog trainer; subplot—Macon's sister and his editor; lesser subplot—Macon's brothers). But there is also the upstairs-downstairs novel where the plot and sub-plot are distributed among social classes (*Don Quixote* is a good example—Quixote and his servant Sancho Panza have parallel plots with divergent outcomes; Tobias Smollett followed Cervantes—see his novel *Humphrey Clinker* where the contrast is between Squire Bramble and his sister and their servants; a good modern instance is John Fowles' *The French Lieutenant's Woman*). And a group of friends or schoolmates or army buddies can provide the same opportunities (e.g., Mary McCarthy's *The Group*). The advantage of the near relations between characters on plot and subplot lines is that they can interact with and observe one another naturally. This mutual awareness creates opportunities for thematic commentary that cuts both ways.

There is one interesting variation on the subplot that gives some people trouble. This is the structure sometimes called first-person biographical narrative. Examples include Conrad's *Heart of Darkness*, Fitzgerald's *The Great Gatsby*, and John le Carré's *The Russia House*. In these texts, the first-person narrator (Marlow, Nick Carraway, and George Smiley, respectively) is telling someone else's story. But in each case, the first-person narrator, the point-of-view character, has a story also, and this story is related to the main plot as a subplot. There is an interesting element of gradation here. The subplot characters are not as passionately given to their desires as their main plot counterparts, not as driven to extremes. Thus Nick Carraway admires Daisy but will never achieve Gatsby's fatal obsessiveness (and seems diminished for it); Marlow follows Kurtz into the jungle but his common sense prevents him from falling for the seductions of power (at the end, having flown too close to the sun, Kurtz dies; Marlow almost dies); and while his agent risks his life in Soviet Russia to rescue the woman he loves, George Smiley, safe in England, can't summon the passion to save his own marriage. The inner story and the outer story resonate with each other because they have similar structures.

This element of gradation is a fairly common aspect of the relationship between plot and subplot.

In any case, writing a novel involves weaving back and forth between plot and subplot. You can invent more than one subplot. You can have more or less text devoted to a subplot. You can and should probably have direct contacts between people on the plot and people on the subplot. For learning about subplot, I send people to Tolstoy, or to *Wuthering Heights*, or to *The Accidental Tourist*. It's important when teaching yourself (by reading) how to handle subplots to find the exact points at which main plot text shifts to subplot text and back again. Only in this way will you become aware of the range of variation in the subplot structure.

Theme

I define theme as a general useable statement of the author's belief about the world and human nature. A theme is useable if it incorporates a statement of human desire and a further statement about how the world works to thwart or interfere with that desire. A phrase like "the conflict between men and women" is not a thematic statement because it doesn't talk about yearning and resistance. There is a sense in which talking about theme this way always takes me back to Freud and his mythic conception of the struggle between the Pleasure Principle and the Reality Principle. In a sense, every novel, at its thematic base, is the story of a human infant encountering the grim reality of other wills, scarcity, work, choice, loss and evil. Every plot focuses on the disconnect between the self and the world.

There are many ways of arriving at a theme. You can buy one off the rack, which is basically what you do when you choose to write a genre novel. Or you can find something topical in the journalistic sociology of the day. Often authors who do this write novels without ever thinking about theme. But it seems to me the best themes evolve out of deeply held personal beliefs. One generally arrives at theme over a period of time and thought, usually focused on the material the author has chosen to work with, that is, the novel itself. Sometimes theme doesn't become clear for several drafts. To arrive at your theme (if you're not lucky enough to figure out what you are doing right away), you need to ask yourself over and over: what does this material illustrate to me about what I believe to be the way the world works? The key here is that you have to arrive at some rock-bottom belief of your own—it doesn't have to be right, to agree with modern therapeutic or sociological theory or be politically or statistically correct or jibe with what your mother told you when you were three. It just has to be something you believe, rather than something you've been taught or told to believe.

You then enunciate your theme in the text of your novel and repeat it over and over—not verbatim but in various forms and from different points of view. Obviously, the plot/subplot structure of the novel gives plenty of opportunity for this in dialogue or in novel thought: characters thinking about their own situations, characters observing and commenting on characters on other plot lines. And obviously, it helps if you have invented a narrating consciousness that is capable of enunciating the theme without sounding out of voice. The passage of novel thought from *Lucky Jim* quoted above is a fair example of novel thought rising to the level of a thematic statement. Here is a lively thematic moment from Saul Bellow's *Henderson the Rain King*. Notice the essential temporal plasticity of novel thought. Henderson is wandering among the tribes of Africa, but part of this moment is remembering and reinterpreting a much earlier scene in the novel with his wife.

> I put my fist to my face and looked at the sky, giving a short laugh and thinking, Christ! What a person to meet at this distance from home. Yes, travel is advisable. And,

believe me, the world is a mind. Travel is mental travel. I had always suspected this. What we call reality is nothing but pedantry. I need not have had that quarrel with Lily, standing over her in our matrimonial bed and shouting until Ricey took fright and escaped with the child. I proclaimed I was on better terms with the real than she was. Yes, yes, yes. The world of facts is real, all right, and not to be altered. The physical is all there, and it belongs to science. But then there is the noumenal department, and there we create and create and create. As we tread our anxious ways, we think we know what is real. And I was telling the truth to Lily after a fashion. I knew it better, all right, but I knew it because it was mine—filled, flowing, and floating with my resemblances; as hers was with *her* resemblances. Oh, what a revelation! Truth spoke to me. To *me*, Henderson!

The general human desire of the theme should be connected clearly with the specific concrete desire of the main character, that is, the concrete desire of the main character (who, in the simplest model, is also the point-of-view character) should be a particular instance of the general desire. The concrete desire defines the plot question that begins the novel and structures its plot arc. The structure of the plot arc is repeated or contrasted in the subplots. In this way, the novel, with its desire, question, plot, thought and subplot(s) in proper relation, will throughout reflect a consistent pattern of ideas or theme. It will have unity, coherence, focus and resonance.

Image Patterning

Now add to this some sense of how image patterning works. An image is something available to sensory apprehension that can be inserted into a piece of writing in the form of words. (The structure I describe also extends to idea patterning—e.g., the ideas of lightness and darkness in Kundera's *The Unbearable Lightness of Being*—or word patterning in which the words refer to concepts instead of sensory images—e.g., in her novel *The Quest for Christa T.*, Christa Wolf constructs an elaborate pattern based on words such as "measure" and "sickness.") An image pattern is a pattern of words and/or meanings created by the repetition of an image. The image can be manipulated or "loaded" to extend the pattern by: 1) the addition of a piece of significant history, 2) association and/or juxtaposition, and 3) ramification or "splintering" and "tying-in." "Splintering" means splitting off some secondary image associated with the main or root image and repeating it as well. "Tying-in" means to write sentences in which you bring the root and the split-off image back together again.

Some authors get very good at tying-in. I've managed to bring as many as three and even four patterns back together in the same sentence. For example, on the last page of *The Life and Times of Captain N.*, my character Oskar writes: "Sometimes I dream there are only the Masks. I walk in a Forest of Trees carved with Masks, a Forest of Masks. Then a roaring, gibbering, whirling Wind comes & sweeps them away." The running patterns are "mask," "forest," "whirl," and "wind." In my novel *Elle*, I wrote: "I pack meat in a rolled-up sealskin, along with Itslk's stone knife, skin drum, lamp and bear statue, a tinder box and Leon's tennis ball, throw on my feather bags, fasten the bearskin over my shoulders with a couple of bone pins, and strap two tennis racquets to my feet, for the snow is still deep among the trees." This sentence ties in three major running patterns: bear, tennis ball, tennis racquets, as well as a couple of lesser ones.

Image patterning gives a novel: 1) a sense of "strangeness" which works against verisimilitude and is a factor in the so-called "poetry" of the piece; 2) an echo effect, a repetitive quality which creates a kind of "story memory," which, like the structural repetition in subplotting, helps give the reader the sense that the book is a coherent world; 3) a rhythm; and 4) a root system that promotes organic unity (the threads connecting the pattern in the text are like the roots of a tree holding the soil together). A boss image is a species or subset of image patterning in which a single overarching image controls the meaning of the story. Margaret Atwood's novel *Cat's Eye* is a good example of this. Elaine Risley's cat's-eye marble is the root image that controls the figurative meaning of the novel. Symbols are simply images that have been loaded with meaning. By loading, again, I mean the process by which a writer adds to and extends the meaning of the bare image. An image which is not repeated and/or loaded is mere incidental description. But in great writing, there is very little that can be classed as mere description. Image patterning, loading and repetition are basic principles in the generation and control of narrative material.

For a quick example of how point of view, plot, subplot, theme and image pattern function in a particular work look at my Revolutionary War novel *The Life and Times of Captain N.* It is constructed by weaving together three parallel plots (a variation of the plot/subplot structure), each with a different point of view: the Loyalist Captain Hendrick Nellis, his son Oskar, and a girl named Mary Hunsacker. The concrete desire of all three is to go home (they have been displaced from their homes by the American Revolution). The question of the novel is: will they get home? The answer for Hendrick is no, but he'll build a copy, an imitation home in Canada, which is what he's doing when he dies. The answer for Oskar is no; he'll reluctantly end up in Canada after the Revolution. The answer for Mary is that she's adaptable; she makes a new home for herself among the Mississauga Indians in Canada, but then loses that as well.

The theme of the book is that contact with the Other (race, language, gender) creates a zone of marginality in which the rules by which we identify ourselves become confused—hence, it is a zone of freedom and loss. The natural human reaction is to want to retreat to identity (represented by the concrete image "home"). But there is also part of us that yearns for that zone of confusion, for difference and otherness, for love and freedom. The theme is conveyed through the actions of the characters as the war forces them out of their homes into the inter-zone of the forest where they live among Indians. In their thoughts (novel thought) the characters mull over what's happened to them and what they plan to do, but the three points of view are quite distinct—each approaches the thematic material from a different angle. Angry at the betrayals of history, Hendrick finds he likes Indians better than his own people and embraces the painful passage into Otherness on his deathbed. Oskar, who wants to be a modern American and writes chatty letters to George Washington, registers panic and discomfort but is the primary narrator, the writer of all the words. And Mary falls in love with the Indian boy who tries to kill her with his death maul; becoming someone new is not so difficult for her. Novel thought also extends into a fourth narrative element, a series of essay fragments entitled "from Oskar's Book about Indians" which are more or less lengthy aphorisms contrasting white European culture and Native American culture. (Once you understand the basic principles of novel thought, the structure can be expanded in all sorts of ways.)

Finally the theme is also bodied forth in a cluster of images and concepts—border, frontier, margin, translation—that spread throughout the book. The root image pattern of the novel is the Whirlwind Mask, an ancient Iroquois mask that is divided down the middle, one side painted black, the other red. A picture of the mask painted on a rock is the first thing Hendrick sees at the beginning of the novel. He recognizes it immediately as the image of the migraine headaches he suffers which he ties (in novel thought) directly to the multiplicity of languages (the otherness) in his head and the chaos of the war. Everyone in the novel ends up with some version of this split superimposed on his or her face. And the image splinters and ramifies into multiple ongoing lines: whirlwind, whirl, wind, mask, face (the Iroquois word for "death" is "without a face"), shadow, forest (when a character carves a series of masks into living trees), and split, among others.

The final picture of the novel, when all these devices are working together, is an organized unity, a kind of total awareness within the novel itself of its own agenda, its parts, its themes and structures and patterns which are woven back and forth through its fabric.

HOW TO WRITE
A SHORT STORY

NOTES ON STRUCTURE
AND AN EXERCISE

Prologue

I N EVERY STORY, there is a tension between formal requirements and the imaginative play required on the part of the
writer to fill the aesthetic spaces created by form with surprising variations and developments. The impassioned inter-
play of form and imagination is what gives the sense of organic
development. Form creates a structure that seems necessary and
logical. The imaginative variation and development of material
in the gaps opened up by form make the story seem alive and
unplanned. Art is a strange and paradoxical thing. Out of these
apparently opposed and antithetical elements, it creates beauty,
meaning and the illusion of living characters.

The following notes and exercise are based on a short story
class I often give when I teach writing. The notes are a primer
for the exercise, and the exercise is not meant to produce a short
story but to demonstrate some basic formal and rhythmic elements that go into writing short stories (as well as to short circuit
some habitual student-writer pathologies). Taken together,

they don't amount to an essay, nor do they aspire to completeness. Though I try to cram in as much technical information as I
can, they barely scratch the surface of all the technical information available to writers in literature itself. Though I tend sometimes to speak with the authority of an enthusiast, this is hardly
meant to be Holy Writ. What I want is for would-be writers to
listen to what I say and then read great stories and see how the
models I propose play out in practice. Everything here is meant
to make you think about form—and then you make your own
discoveries, teach yourself. I'd like all of us to become better,
more appreciative readers and for our writing to grow out of
that.

Story Defined

A short story is a narrative involving a conflict between two
poles (A vs B). This conflict needs to develop through a series of
actions in which A and B get together again and again and again
(three is a good number to start with, but there can be more).
Or, another definition I use: by a story I mean a narrative that extends through a set of articulations, events or event sequences, in
which the central conflict is embodied once, and again, and again
(three is the critical number here—looking back at the structure
of folk tales), such that in these successive revisitings we are
drawn deeper into the soul or moral structure of the story. These
successive articulations of the conflict give the story a rhythmic,
surging quality. A story is written or a narrative surface is constructed with two concerns in mind: 1) the need to satisfy expectation, that is the need to fulfill the requirements of form, and
I believe literature is a process of thinking with its own peculiar
form, which the reader has come to know without consciously
knowing it; and 2) the need to create interest, i.e. interest within
the text, through variation of form, surprising turns or denials
of expectation, dramatic action and emotional resonance.

Conflict is any relationship of opposition. If I want to hold your hand and you don't want me to, that's conflict. If you want to sleep in tomorrow morning and you have to go to the dentist at 8:30 a.m., that's conflict. If you love Andrea and Beatrice and yet believe in monogamous relationships, that's conflict. If you want to get a tan and it's raining, that's conflict. If the Russians send a missile over, that's conflict. If you want someone to cuddle you but can't stand your husband, that's conflict. If you're worried about your job prospects next year, that's conflict. Conflict is ubiquitous. In a story you simply pick one, focus on it, and allow it to eventuate into action again and again and again.

A and B can be characters in conflict with each other or competing forces within a single character. Sometimes a character is wrestling internally, and sometimes one character is wrestling with another and, sometimes, also, a character can wrestle with natural forces or an institution or whatever; the definition is not meant to be limiting in this regard. Literature is a way of thinking by pushing characters through a set of actions. It is very difficult to go deeper into the intimate emotions of a character without in some way testing that character in a series of scenes that involve the same conflict.

The key word here is "same." Basically, in a short story you trap your character (A) in a cage with a rat (B). The character and the rat fight each other, rest, fight again, try to figure out how to beat each other, rest, fight again, and so on till the character wins, the rat wins, they resolve things, or they declare an armistice and get out of the cage together. Characters are forced to go deeper into themselves at the points in the story where they have to look at themselves and the other character in a new way, so that they can somehow get out of the rat-box. The exigencies of form force depth and change on a character. In this way, form drives content.

Are A and B really poles, meaning opposites, or does any kind of difference work? Well, they are not "opposites" in the sense of antonyms. They are opposite as in opposing actions or intentions; they interfere with each other. Keep the verbs in the sentences. But obviously these opposing intentions or actions can be quite various. So in a sense any sort of "difference" can initiate intention, action, opposition and conflict. I like blue, you like red, and we need to paint the living room. It doesn't seem quite accurate to say my liking blue and your liking red are "opposites." But this is what I am talking about. And I use the word "pole" to indicate the loci of opposition. And again these poles can be all sorts of things (see above).

How does action bring them together? You can understand how an "action" might bring two people together again and again but it's less easy to see how two sides of a person's desire mechanism might be brought together again and again. Once again this is actually quite simple when you realize that we are talking about conflicting desires and actions not opposite ideas. Actions and desires are not contradictory—they are in opposition; conflict is not contradiction; and a character first acts on one impulse and then the other, goes forward, retreats, reels back, makes compromises with necessity, concedes a position out of politeness, ponders his own reactions, realizes that he prefers disorderly love to antiseptic order and changes his behavior.

This definition of short story form can be rendered somewhat mathematically as $((GOAL=DESIRE)+CONFLICT+(SERIES\ OF\ INSTANCES\ OF\ CONFLICT=BACKBONE=PLOT))=(STRUCTURE=FORM)$. This formula does not constitute a complete description of a story or the possibilities of a story, but it tentatively blocks out the basic motive and event structure. There are still what I call ancillary devices, which are no less essential to the composition of a story.

I know this story definition may feel artificial, but it outlines a structure that has the advantage of opening up what I call aesthetic space. Form feels initially as if it shuts down creative freedom, but it actually does the opposite by creating a number of blank spaces or cells or chunks of aesthetic space (globs, see below) in which the writer is forced to create new conflict material. In effect, if you have to write three interesting scenes between the same two people on the same conflict line, you are willy-nilly forced to vary the conflicts in a dramatic and interesting way and you are forced to go deeper into the moral and spiritual implications of the conflict and the relationships. In other words, form forces you to go deeper and be more creative, not the opposite.

What one finds, working with student stories, is that people learning to write violate formal expectations in fairly consistent ways. Common student mistakes include: a) the partial story— a couple of thousand words, give or take, which introduce a situation and a conflict but which end after the first major scene; the story doesn't develop through a series of actions; b) the broken-back story—the student loses confidence in his/her ability to move the conflict forward and shifts to another conflict; c) the bathtub story—a story which takes place almost completely as backfill in the mind of a single character (who often spends the whole narrative sitting in a bathtub—I am only being slightly facetious); d) the victim story—the student fails to generate true conflict because the protagonist refuses to speak up for himself, fight back, take a stand, get angry, etc. (These observations about failed student stories lead to the following also slightly facetious rule of thumb: good stories are about obsessive-compulsive characters, failed stories are about passive-aggressive characters.)

"The Dead," A Reality Check

But now, as a kind of reality check, let's look at James Joyce's "The Dead." I choose "The Dead" for analysis because once a student brought it to me and said it disproved all my arguments about form. He said it was a story without form. The student was making a common error, mistaking a variation of form with formlessness. When you are reading and analyzing for form and structure you need to be able to identify a basic device and compare and contrast the ways different writers deploy it. What new variations, inversions, wrinkles, does any given writer use to make the device fresh?

"The Dead" is built on a structure of three conflicts between Gabriel, the protagonist, and women, a different woman in each case, with the story of his mother looming in the background (and past time) as a shadow fourth. This is a crucial variation of conventional form. Instead of having Gabriel in conflict with his wife over and over again, Joyce puts him through the same confrontation with three different women: Lily, the serving girl; Miss Ivors, the journalist; and Gretta, his wife. In each case, Gabriel oversteps by assuming things (feelings, thoughts, desires) that don't exist—he's a typical bourgeois male. In each case, the woman snaps back, puts him (almost comically) in his place. Then he becomes flustered, loses his composure (Joyce uses the word "gloom" to describe Gabriel's state of mind), fusses with his clothes, worries about the speech he is to give at dinner. He rights himself and, by ritual acts of male dominance and condescension, regains his composure,. He gives Lily money and then turns round and condescends to Gretta, joking about how foolish she is over golashes. After his contretemps with Miss Ivors, he unctuously offers to walk her home (asserting his prerogative as a male protector) and then patronizes her new ideas in his speech.

The third reiteration of the conflict, with Gretta, takes a different turn. Gabriel becomes romantically aroused when he mistakenly jumps to the conclusion that she is thinking of him (as men often do—we are a self-absorbed lot) when she is merely thinking (actually thinking of someone else). Then he goes through a comic cycle of gloom, anger, passionately masterful sexual desire (you know, all thoughtful women need is a good fuck). After which, he finally "sees" her. Somehow, by telling him the story of Michael Furey's love death, Gretta breaks through Gabriel's protective rituals and attitudes. She cracks him open. He "sees" her and, in seeing her, is able to imagine a different sort of love, different from the domestic convention ("the years of dull existence") he has been following. And he can begin his own "journey to the west."

A middle-aged version of the youthful protagonist in Joyce's other great love story "Araby," Gabriel wants to get the girl, which, in symbolic terms, means love. But every time he interacts with a woman, he comes smack up against the inhibitions of his own learned behaviour and the social conventions of his era and class. Walking into the story, he merely wants to appear suave, successful and masterful, which are the facsimiles of love he has learned to settle for. In stories, character is perversion; what a character wants is often a fetish, an object that bears some metonymic or synecdochic or associative relationship to what he really desires. So the plot of "The Dead" can be represented something like this: (A wants love but his habitual relations with women prevent him from achieving anything but a conventional and insecure mastery)+$((A \times B_1)+(A \times B_2)+(A \times B_3))$. Each woman is more important to Gabriel than the previous one. Each comes closer to threatening and overturning his core psychic constructs. And each woman confronts him with the truth.

The Theory of Globs

Also consider what I call the Theory of Globs. I invented the Theory of Globs when I was somewhat younger and trying to teach myself to write by reading how-to books. Over and over, I encountered the idea that narrative prose can be divided into scene and summary, or scene, summary and exposition, or scene,

summary, exposition and description. I happily went about trying to write stories with scenes followed by exposition and summary followed by scenes, and they all turned out lumpy and
awkward. I looked at books I loved only to find that real writers
didn't seem to write like that. It was very difficult to tease
apart a lump of summary when in fact good writers often thread
summary and exposition and character thought through their
scenes or insert mini-scenes and quoted bits of dialogue in their
exposition. Good writing seemed more like a dance as opposed
to a lumpy procession of bits of text typed by function.

So I tried to figure out another way of breaking a narrative
text into segments. Narrative is about the movement of characters through time. Good writers continuously employ time-
switch devices to keep the flow of time orderly, that is, so that we
know when something is taking place relative to other events in
the story. (For example, time-indicating phrases—"one day,"
"the next day," "an hour later," "at 9 a.m. on Tuesday"—as well
as adverbs, conjunctions, time and date stamp subheads, line or
chapter breaks, and tense changes.) I noticed that narrative time
moves ahead in jumps, with chunks of text between the jumps.
These chunks of text might be scene, summary or exposition or
more probably a quicksilver mix of all three, but all the stuff in a
given chunk of text takes place at the same time. Thus I began to
see that time chunks were far more important in determining
how a narrative text flows than the function of the individual
bits of text. In the interests of keeping myself entertained, I
called these text chunks "globs."

Globs then are chunks of information (fancy name: semantic
units). They can be scenic, descriptive or panoramic or serve
any number of other narrative functions. Operationally, globs
are more often than not defined by time shifts. That is, if you
read a story or a novel, more often than not, time indicators
("before," "after," "once," "a day later," line breaks, etc.) or

tense changes signal a movement between globs. A scene would be a single glob. A section of backfill would be another. (The time-shift principle doesn't apply universally. More discursive writers like Sterne or Kundera will simply shift sideways and slip into a different subject matter or train of thought.)

Thinking in terms of globs gives you a more or less quantitative approach to controlling certain aspects of narrative flow. For example, basic rules of proportion apply: the longer the globs the slower the narrative movement. The shorter the globs the quicker the movement. This is a root consideration in that mysterious literary notion of pace. Pace is the speed of movement through a sequence of globs. Usually an author indicates in the first few lines of a story or novel what the pace will be and sticks to it. A long glob in the middle of a short-globbed story is clearly a faux pas or, at best, an anomaly that may need rethinking—it might, for example, be shortened or split up (running globs). There is an obvious, but useful, corollary in regard to emphasis: the longer treatment (glob) always seems more important (to the reader) than the shorter. And, similarly, a repeated treatment is more important than a single instance.

Globs are modular. Think of the way newspaper editors once actually cut stories into segments with scissors and pasted them back together again in a new order. This can be done just as easily with fiction. Globs can be repeated. Or, once entered in the text, they may be referred to over and over, bringing the whole back into the reader's mind without necessarily going through the entire sequence of words again. Globs may be organized in patterns of light and dark (comedy and tragedy) or in patterns of increasing poetic intensity (rising to a climax). This repetition and patterning, combined with globbing (yes, there is a verb "to glob") for pace, helps to give a piece of writing a rhythmic quality. There can be globs within globs (nested globs). They can be varied as to length so as to give an effect of syncopation. Writing becomes a dance, a glittering flash of movement, instead of that awkward shuffle of scene, summary and description.

On Story Openings

When you open a story, think back to first principles—expectation (form) and interest and the subsidiary problem of establishing complexity and amplitude in the narrative voice. What do these first principles then require in an opening? They require: 1) an identifiable point of view; 2) probably at least two characters; 3) a conflicted situation involving the two characters; 4) a mode of presentation (language, sentences, paragraphs) that is strong and interesting besides. There is a kind of sentence structure which can often give you all this at once. I call it the but-construction, that is a sentence (or paragraph) that turns on the word "but" or some cognate, or an implied "but," antithesis, irony, or contrasting parallel. To put it another way, a but-construction occurs when one proposition is followed by another that is a contrast, contrary, antithesis or somehow runs counter to expectation. The two propositions pivot on a "but" or implied "but." The effect is the creation of conflict at the level of a sentence (or paragraph); it creates interest, drama, and action at the level of propositions.

If you look at how I sometimes open stories, you'll see an almost stylized opening: "I thought my wife had left me but she is back. What she has been doing the last two years I have no idea." "I am in bed with a woman who looks like a movie star and (implied "but") I have lost my memory." "My wife and I decide to separate, and then (implied "but") suddenly we are almost happy together." Often these openings are written separately, without any idea on my part of who the characters are, where the plot is going, i.e. with no story in mind, only an idea of the formal requirements and the need to create interest and complexity at the outset. You can then extrapolate from this and look for the but-constructions all through the work, whole paragraphs or sequences constructed around patterns of but-constructions which take on the character of riffs in a piece of jazz—i.e. the form demands it, the requirement of interest demands it.

Image Patterns

An image is something available to sensory apprehension, or an idea, as in Kundera, that can be inserted into a piece of writing in the form of a word or words. An image pattern is a pattern of words and/or meanings created by the repetition of an image. The image can be manipulated or "loaded" to extend the pattern by 1) by adding a piece of significant history, 2) by association and/or juxtaposition, and 3) by ramifying or "splintering" and "tying-in." Splintering means splitting off some secondary image associated with the main or root image and repeating it as well. Tying-in means to write sentences in which you bring the root and the split-off image back together again. Image patterning gives a story 1) a sense of "strangeness" which is against verisimilitude and is a factor in the so-called literariness of the piece, 2) an echo-chamber effect (or internal memory—important for giving the reader a sense that there is a coherent world of the book), 3) a rhythm, and 4) a root or web effect that promotes organic unity (the threads connecting the pattern in the text are like the roots of a tree holding the soil together). A boss image is a species or subset of repeating image in which a single overarching image controls the meaning of the story. Symbols are simply images that are loaded. By loading, again, I mean the process by which a writer adds to and extends the meaning of the bare image. An image that is not loaded is incidental or mere description. But in great writing, there is very little that can be classed as mere description. Images, loading and repetition are basic principles in the generation and control of narrative material.

As an example of image patterning, consider my short story "Why I Decide to Kill Myself and Other Jokes." The root image is the jar of cyanide the female protagonist steals from a lab, intending to use it to kill herself. The word cyanide, the jar of cyanide, and the chemical symbol (KCN) repeat throughout the story. Cyanide is a white crystal, which in the story is associated with snow (obviously another white crystal). So there is a pattern of snow words and a glass globe shake-up and, of course, the story has to take place in winter (in this way, form drives content). Cyanide is used in making the paint colour Prussian blue and it turns people blue (cyanosis). So the word "blue" splits off from the main pattern and takes on a life of its own inside the story. "Blue" is the last word in the story. And there, it's a pun, the meaning of which washes back over the story, doubling all the original meanings. This web of word and image patterns forms a structure that, simultaneous with the forward-moving plot structure of the story, resonates with it and shapes its meaning.

Repetition: Subplots, Doubles, Recycling and Juggling

Repetition is the heart of narrative art, and if you don't read texts with a pencil and note the repetitions, there is no way you'll learn how they work. (Virginia Woolf says in her diary that she can't understand how people read at all without a pencil in their hands.) In the foregoing, I talked about large structural repetition and image patterning. I've mentioned word repetition and parallelism. Stories can also borrow the novelistic device of the subplot. Alice Munro, for example, rarely limits herself to a simple story line. She constructs branching lines or subplots by creating foils and doubles for her characters. In the long story called "Lives of Girls and Women" in the book with the same title, the protagonist, Del, has a friend, Naomi, who has a plot that forms a criss-cross pattern with Del's main plot. As Del moves toward sexual initiation with the middle-aged Mr. Chamberlain, the sexy Naomi falls sick and recovers as a sort of born-again puritan. Del's mother spawns a double, her boarder, Fern, and Fern and Mr. Chamberlain have a seedy little plot together, the opposite of the staid, middle class, proto-feminist uprightness of Del's mother.

The main action (the desire-resistance pattern) is the sexual plot between Del and Chamberlain—the story proceeds in a series of steps that involve their relationship. But then Munro will spend time on other off-plot elements—Del and Naomi walking through town (sex theme comes in with the peacocks), the brothel paragraph, the incident with Naomi's father and the Bible story about virgins, etc. Each of these segments stays on topic (sex) but also expands into a religious armature, social class armature, and so on. Some segments are tied to the main plot both thematically and as subplots, some are merely tied to the main plot thematically. Munro is not trying to write an essay on sex in small-town Ontario. She knows that a story develops branches and that these branches create echo effects, resonances, that are important to the meaning of the story—a meaning which is complex and mysterious. (It's worth noting that Munro seems to have what amounts to an instinct for doubling. She rarely leaves a character alone in a sentence let alone a whole paragraph. Fern and Del's mother get described (and contrasted) together—because that makes a more dramatic description—description becomes story, and the two characters come alive.)

Recycling and juggling are terms I use somewhat loosely to describe another ancillary compositional process in story writing. Stories have a linear component based on the forward movement of plot and time. But the stuff, the textured density of material draped over this bare bone of plot, often takes on a churning, recursive quality. Words, thematic topics or motifs, images and memories start up and then recycle through the story, coming back again and again, with variation. This process creates a certain imaginative economy: a story isn't five thousand words, all different, all moving the plot forward. In many stories, much of the material is used again and again. A rule of thumb: during composition, when a gap opens up and the story seems to resist moving forward, reach back into the earlier text of the story, find something to bring in again and proceed from there. This recycling or juggling of a basic set of materials contributes to the overall effect of unity and coherence in the story.

Thematic Passages

The fear of being too obvious is a common failing of inexperienced short story writers. Excessive obliquity leads straight to the purgatory of vagueness. In every class I teach there will be at least one student who believes he has put the idea of purity into a story because someone is wearing white. Students speckle their stories with symbols, clues and hints instead of saying what they mean and telling the reader how to read the story. They want to be interpreted (the effect of too many English literature classes) instead of being read. An antidote to this interpretive fallacy is to adopt as a rule of thumb the principle that if you want the reader to think of a word when he reads your story, put the word in the story. If the story is about love, the word "love" should occur several times in the story (tellingly, the majority of student relationship stories I've seen manage to avoid using the word at all). If you want the story to be passionate, use the word "passion."

The truth is that good stories often open themselves up to readers by reading themselves. A thematic passage is any text in which the narrator or some other character questions or offers an interpretation of the action of the story. Characters in the story explore the meaning of the story by asking questions of their own impulses and actions. The act of questioning is more important here than the act of answering. One of the most common devices of thematic inquiry in fiction (mostly ignored by beginners) is the rhetorical question. The questions don't have to be answered, or they don't have to be answered correctly. But by asking the question in the text, the author creates a sense that the story is aware of the larger mysteries of its own existence. A story that does not ask its own questions often seems to be fatally unaware of itself, unintelligent and inhibited. It cannot develop any moral or psychological depth. By asking questions the story generalizes it own meaning, opens up thematic depths and, more importantly, creates new possibilities of action.

Two other lovely little devices for inserting thematic material in a short story are dreams and aphorisms. Dreams in fiction are never like dreams in real life. Fictional dreams have a point; they reflect and comment on some other structure in the story. When a character dreams and, on waking, interprets or questions his dream, he is, by association, doing thematic work on the story itself.

Aphorisms are short, pithy, somewhat artificial statements; they often seem arrogant and dogmatic, but the very artificiality, elegance and wit of an aphorism draws its content into question. They are actually stylized forms of thought, or conjecture, mostly constructed on the contrast of opposites (obliquity and vagueness in the aphorism I used at the opening of this section of the essay). There are several common aphoristic structures. For example:

> There are two positions available to us—either crime which renders us happy, or the noose, which prevents us from being unhappy. – *de Sade*

There are two kinds of readers—the adventurers who glory in the breathtaking audacity and risk of a well-turned aphorism and the wienies who, lacking courage themselves, find it an affront in others. *– Glover*

The world is but a school of inquiry. *– Montaigne*

Love is an erotic accident prolonged to disaster. *– Glover*

"There are only three things to be done with a woman," said Clea once. "You can love her, suffer for her, or turn her into literature." *– Durrell*

Three people become famous as a result of any new artistic movement: the one who invents it, the one who does it best, and the one who parodies it. *– Glover*

Writing Dialogue

I have a few rules of thumb for writing dialogue:

1) It's helpful to say to yourself that dialogue in a story is not like dialogue in real life. Real life dialogue wanders, loops, stops, digresses and picks up subjects from a hundred other conversations. You can't do that in a story. Dialogue in a story is highly organized; it's a form of action and, as such, it must contain drama and conflict and motivation.

2) Often in writing a story it is worthwhile to consider ways of avoiding fully-realized dialogue scenes that are not on the direct conflict line. Often subordinate dialogue scenes can be implied with a couple of lines or less of summary and a single snippet of speech in quotation marks. Alternatively you can use free indi-

rect discourse or reported dialogue to avoid a full-scale scene. All of these techniques promote narrative speed and concision and can be used to vary the standard student three-to-five-pages-of-dialogue scene.

3) Dialogue is often more lively and interesting if it uses a technique I call "not-answering," that is if the speeches from one character to the next are in conflict and do not simply go pit-a-pat like a friendly ping-pong rally. There are various ways of not-answering in dialogue. Some are:

   a) Silence: Silence can be a great dramatic tool in dialogue (see my story "Story Carved in Stone" for an example, or the opening scenes of the movie *Paris, Texas*). "Do you love me, Jack?" Jack says nothing.

   b) Lying: "Do you love me, Jack?" "No," he said, lying to her, lying to himself.

   c) Repeating the words of the previous speech: "I love you, Jack." "I love you, Jack. What does that mean?" he asked. (This is a favourite David Mamet device.)

   d) Talking at cross-purposes: "Jack, I love you. I've been waiting all day—" "Sweetheart, did Amy Goodis leave any messages for me?" "I just wanted to say . . . Amy Goodis? Yes, I guess. She called twice." She pauses. "Is Amy—? Oh, I see."

   e) Argument: "Jack, I love you." "No you don't. You never loved anybody but that stupid Pomeranian."

   f) Answering with a question: "I love you, Jack." "Do you?"

There are more ways of not-answering, but you can see that each implies two motivations. One character wants something; the other character wants something else that is in conflict. These techniques create interesting dialogue and scene-plotting.

It's fun to string several of these techniques into a dialogue sequence and discover where the dialogue takes the plot and not vice versa (that is, let the form dictate content). Also you should study dialogue in your reading now and spot the various techniques as they come up.

An Exercise, or How to Write a Modern Short Story in One Easy Lesson

Okay, now here is an exercise. This is meant to be a rough template of a minimal story trajectory. It is meant to simplify and incorporate many of the devices and structures discussed in the preceding notes. If you follow the template correctly, keeping in mind the formal lessons above, you will end up with a narrative that looks something like a contemporary short story. (Note that the line breaks function as rough globbing lines, separating the text into time units and emphasizing the modular nature of narrative structure.) On the other hand, rather than simply trying out the exercise, a better idea would be to use the formal lessons and the exercise template as reading tools, that is, as ways of identifying formal structures in successful short stories. But if you prefer the lazy approach, start this way:

1) Write a 2-3 sentence opening in which two characters in some relationship with each other are caught in some odd present ongoing situation. This can be comic or violent or tragic. Use a but-construction to make the set-up grammatically dramatic. Keep the point of view structures simple: pick one character to be the protagonist and point of view and stick to it. Use the word "worry" somewhere.

LINE BREAK

(In a short story, you might not use line breaks to differentiate various plot steps and/or thematic material, but it's useful to see how easily one can move forward in a narrative with a little skip and a time-switch word.)

2) Write a small scene with these two characters (don't add extra characters, do not go back in time). The scene begins with the time-switch phrase "One day. . . ." Use some narration but rely mainly on dialogue to carry the scene. Use the not-answering strategies to make the dialogue dramatic. Include the words "laughter" and "tears." Keep it short.

LINE BREAK

3) Write another small scene with the same two characters (don't add extra characters, do not go back in time). The scene begins with the time-switch phrase "The next morning . . ." (so it clearly follows the previous scene). Use some narration but rely again mostly on dialogue. Don't drift into backfill (at all—if I seem to repeat myself on this point, well . . .). Use the word "passion" somewhere.

LINE BREAK

4) Write a thematic passage (3-5 sentences) in which your main character, the character whose head you are in, speculates on what is happening in the story, the nature of the conflict between the two characters, the nature of the situation, etc. Try using the device of the rhetorical question to get this revery going. Literally, you can ask the question "What is this story about?" Include the words "love" and "blood."

LINE BREAK

5) Write another scene with the same two characters. The scene begins with the time-switch phrase "That night. . . ." Again, rely mostly on dialogue. Begin to repeat some words or ideas from previous sections. Try to achieve a climax, a high level of conflict and intensity.

LINE BREAK

6) Write a second thematic passage inquiring into the nature of what's now happened. In this section use rhetorical questions again, but you can also (since it follows directly on a scene that takes place at night) use dreams to reflect what's going on. You can have the character inquire into either the dream or the real-life events or both. Try an aphorism.

LINE BREAK

7) Write a final section that begins with the time switch "A week later, so much had happened. . . ." In this section, you'll have to give a brief summary of the week's activities, the intervening action. Then bring the same two characters back together for one more brief dialogue scene. Then end it in a sentence or two. Repeat the words you have begun to repeat elsewhere in the exercise.

ATTACK OF THE COPULA SPIDERS

THOUGHTS ON WRITING WELL IN A POST-LITERATE AGE

The Age of Post-Literacy

AT THE BEGINNING OF *Don Quixote*, the old don, Alonzo the Good, goes insane from reading books, jumps into a rusty suit of armour and dashes off on his nag Rozinante in the name of an imaginary lady, Dulcinea del Toboso. In an effort to cure him, his friends, the curate and the barber, sort through his books, burn some of them and brick up the library doorway to conceal the rest. They tell Quixote that an evil necromancer has done the brickwork. Because he lives in a book, he believes them. In Jane Austen's *Mansfield Park*, Sir Thomas Bertram has to leave home for Antigua to manage his plantations. While he's away his children and their air-headed friends decide to put on a play, the reading of which unleashes a storm of libidinal indiscretion. Arriving just in time, Sir Thomas gathers all the copies of the play and burns them. In Ray Bradbury's science-fiction novel *Fahrenheit 451*, Bradbury imagines an upside-down world in which all books have been banned and the fire department exists for the sole purpose of finding and burning books. The novel's hero, Montag, discovers an underground movement where people memorize books, then destroy them. In order to preserve books from the bookburners, they become the books. But, chillingly, as a character in the book tells Montag, it's not as if the book bans and the firemen were necessary. "The public itself stopped reading of its own accord."

Books used to be seen as a threat, as dangerous articles capable of corrupting morals or inspiring passionate love, igniting revolutions or sewing, variously, liberty, disorder and oppression. Books had to be watched, banned, proscribed, listed, condemned, and bowdlerized. *Ulysses* and *Lady Chatterley's Lover* were put on trial. Henry Miller's work was banned in the United States. But not anymore. Not now. No need to burn or memorize or smuggle books because, in fact, nobody reads them anyway. School boards routinely and quietly choose what classics our children can't read, and nobody cares. English departments study the sociology of texts and excommunicate great works from the canon because they were written by authors of the wrong race and gender, and everyone nods with approval. Because books have become irrelevant. We live in an age of post-literacy. What B. W. Powe defines as "the condition of semi-literacy, where most people can read and write to some extent, but where the literate sensibility no longer occupies a central position in culture, society, and politics. Post-literacy occurs when the ability to comprehend the word decays."

For most of my life I've been in denial about post-literacy, blaming local conditions or my own myriad insufficiencies for anomalies that now appear systemic rather than incidental. Teaching itself helped mask the true conditions and contradictions. I have been teaching creative writing and, occasionally, English literature for a dozen years, and I really thought that all those writing students valued books, language, writing and writers. If they didn't, I told myself, they would after I was finished with them. But over the years it has been born in on me that this is not true.

As I write, we (both in Canada and the United States) are in the midst of a sudden and astonishing proliferation of second-generation low-residency Master of Fine Arts writing programs which themselves are a sort of third-generation elaboration of the old-fashioned Iowa Writers Workshop-style residential Master of Fine Arts programs. Now more than ever it is possible to get a doctorate in creative writing, and it is possible to get degrees in non-fiction writing, editing, playwriting, and screen-writing. And, sad to say, it is possible to obtain any one of these degrees without writing a publishable sentence, paragraph, story, novel or essay.

Going to writing school has become a bit like taking piano and water-colour lessons in the late 19th and early 20th centuries, a popular outward sign of bourgeois cultural accomplishment, a commercially available testimonial of creativity, the public stamp of approval. In other words, we have commodified literary creativity, boxed it and put a price on it. You know how in *The Wizard of Oz*, at the end, the scarecrow gets a diploma. Well, here's your diploma, you are a licensed creator, the equal of Joyce and Homer. But it doesn't mean you can write a book that is publishable, let alone a work of art or, dare we say it, a masterpiece, a classic, that you read with intensity and wisdom, that you love your tools as if they were your children.

There is a beautiful event-sequence in *Anna Karenina* that somewhat illustrates the point. Vronsky and Anna have left Russia and are wandering among the spas and cities of Europe. Vronsky finds an Italian painting professor and begins to do "studies from nature" with that airy enthusiasm he shows for everything from horse racing to Anna. In Italy, he hears of a famous Russian painter in exile, one of the great men of his age. Vronsky wants to go and see the fellow Russian painter, to patronize him, buy his paintings, help with money. But Mikhailov disappoints. The great artist turns out to be gruff, cold, peasantish, and taciturn. He doesn't want to talk about painting, he doesn't want to comment on Vronsky's own artistic efforts, he doesn't want to come to cultural dinner parties. He seems embarrassingly lower class and under-educated. But having seen Mikhailov's paintings, Vronsky quietly abandons painting himself. This is how Tolstoy describes Mikhailov's reaction to Vronsky's art:

> He knew that it was impossible to forbid Vronsky to amuse himself with art; he knew that the count and every other dilettante had a perfect right to paint what they liked, but he could not help feeling vexed. A man could not be forbidden to make himself a big wax doll and to kiss it. But if that man came down and sat with this doll in front of a man in love and began caressing his doll as the lover caressed his beloved, the lover could not help feeling vexed. Mikhailov had the same unpleasant feeling when he saw Vronsky's paintings: he felt amused, vexed, sorry, and offended.

Here's a quiz: How many of you can tell me what a gerund is? How many of you know the difference between a compound and a complex sentence? Better yet how many of you in composing a piece of writing experiment with subordination or inversion to gauge effect? Everyone seems to know how to write a simile but how many consciously experiment with parallel construction, image patterning, puns, aphorisms? How many of you pay any attention to the revision of sentences and paragraphs? How many of you study or even notice the structure of sentences and paragraphs in the work of authors you admire? How many of you consciously and studiously compare the sentences and paragraphs of writers you admire with your own sentences and paragraphs? How many of you make technical notes in the margins, count repetitions, note the elaborations of image patterns on a single page, in a whole work? When was the last time you read a work of literature more than once? More than twice? More than three times? When was the last time you forced yourself through a difficult work that seemed initially unreadable to you though you knew its greatness by reputation? Don't answer.

On Clarity and Correctness

In the post-literate age, here is what I have to teach writing students. Apparently, given the manuscripts I read, at least fifty percent of my students do not know what a dangling modifier is, let alone a split infinitive, a sentence fragment, a pronoun with an ambiguous or missing antecedent, a run-on sentence, a comma splice, or the difference between a comma, a colon and a semicolon. Often they do not know how to punctuate dialogue correctly, or, even if they do, they don't mind being careless about it here and there and letting me make the correction. They write in high-school cliches: "His eyes *scanned* her face"; "Jamie *couldn't believe* she had just been run over by a highway roller and left for dead." Or they have lost their idiomatic English: "I *could* care less about your fecking grammar and punctuation rules" instead of the correct "I *couldn't* care less about. . . ." Apparently, a lot of people don't care about slovenly prose—their own or other students'. Sometimes I keep correcting the same errors on revision after revision. Student writers like this do not seem to suffer shame at their ignorance. In the post-literate age, such ignorance is the norm. Student writers like this do not seem to understand a basic rule of editorial selection: editors read till they come to the first mistake. At least they used to. I am fairly sure now that a lot of editors don't read either. That post-literate culture again.

In a post-literate age, writing means just putting words, any old words, on the page. And reading means only noticing that there are words on the page.

Look, I know what poetic license is and I know how to shade a meaning or withhold a piece of information till the most dramatic point of revelation. But false artfulness is merely portentous, and incorrect grammar is unprofessional, insulting to the reader, and an aesthetic disaster. If I can circle the word "it" five times in two sentences and the word "it" in these sentences refers to five different antecedents, then, at the very least, I can say you've been vague and that you could improve the writing in these sentences by changing the word "it" to a noun or a name. Time and again, I just shake my head and think: listen, X, you are writing while asleep or you just can't read because if you could read you'd know that what you have written here is too garbled to be comprehensible. The first rule of good writing is to be clear. If you don't write what you mean or mean what you write and if your reader can't understand what you mean, you have failed as a writer.

Here is an excerpt from a letter I wrote to a student:

Clarity is the first virtue of good writing. Lack of clarity is not the same as artful use of purposeful ambiguity. What does this sentence mean? "This thinness was a calm one." I puzzled and puzzled over it. This thinness was a calm thinness? What could a "calm thinness" and, for that matter, a not-calm thinness be? What's an agitated thinness? You may mean something precise and interesting, but you have not conveyed your thought to the reader. What does it mean to throw rocks at cows "on a river bed?" A river bed is the ground underneath the flowing water of the river. What would cows be doing there? What does it mean when you write that the girls stretched their legs "across the benches underneath the lockers?" I can only think it must hurt to have those lockers sitting on their legs.

Here is another:

> As I read you more and more, I begin to see that some, at
> least, of your problems develop because of lack of clarity,
> grammar and punctuation issues, and a false artfulness.
> Your penchant for sentence fragments is an instance of
> false artfulness. There just seems to be no reason, most of
> the time, for the fragments, especially when they modify
> the sentence before. The false artfulness is portentous at
> best and vague and confusing at worst. You just can't write
> a successful essay with sentences that are unclear, because
> unclear sentences don't do the work (convey the meaning)
> they are supposed to. That's a minimal requirement of
> the art. If you are clear, then you can begin to bend the
> rules of grammar. But first you need to be absolutely clear.
> The rules of grammar, applied correctly, promote clarity.

Sloppy sentence structure, the over-use and abuse of pro-
nouns, the abuse of the passive voice, the vague or general verb,
the dangling modifier, unattributed dialogue, droning and repetitious sentence structure, these all contribute to lack of clarity.
And on a very simple level, learning to correct these faults will improve your writing (not to mention your thoughts). Yet in the age
of post-literacy it seems that would-be writers often take it for
granted that someone else along the way will know how to clean
up their brilliantly inspired incomprehensible prose. But someone won't. If you don't care about your prose, no one else will.

On Verbs

Beyond the demand for clarity and grammatical correctness,
there are a few rules of thumb that student writers can and

should follow to improve their writing, principles I have been teaching over and over, year after year, apparently, to no effect. They boil down to three basic maxims: 1) use strong, precise, concrete, active verbs and verb forms such as verbal adjectives and gerunds; 2) use contrast and antithesis to create drama (conflict, story) at the level of sentences and paragraphs; 3) learn how to read.

Let's think about verbs. A long time ago, I invented the term "copula spider" to describe a phenomenon I was noticing, time and time again, in bad student writing. Actually I've discovered we don't even call it the copula anymore. "Copula" is too close to "copulate" and thus politically incorrect and unfit for the tender minds of North American teenagers. Evidence again of the post-literate miasma. A copula spider occurs when a student uses the verb "to be" so many times on a page that I can circle all the instances, connect them with lines, and draw a spider diagram. Now there is nothing grammatically wrong with the verb "to be," but if you use it over and over again your prose is likely to be flaccid and uninteresting. The reason is that the verb "to be" is only a linking verb, a connector, something like an (=) equal sign. It does not make a picture or an image. It has no poetry.

All sentences have verbs (apparently, many of my writing students don't seem to know this). Every verb is an opportunity to present, represent or picture an action. The more precise and arresting the action is, the more lively the sentence. Here is what I wrote one student on the subject of copula spiders:

> You're not infusing the page with actions and pictures. The verb "to be" just should NOT be the verb you lean on habitually. Learn automatically to rewrite a percentage of "to be" sentences to active pictureable sentences. "The barn WAS red" should become something like "Ancient red paint peeled off the barn boards leaving them patchy

and leprous-looking, matching the old man's mood as he nailed up the for sale sign and walked away for the last time." The verb "to be" doesn't tell a story."

As I say, there is nothing illegal about the copula, and as you may have noticed, I am using it over and over again in this essay (the reason being that the action of this essay is in making connections between things that are not normally connected, that is, in grouping, linking and defining terms). A useful and necessary verb, the copula only weakens prose with incessant repetition, when the author depends on it too much, in a narrative context. This also applies to the use of the passive voice, a subset of the use of the copula. There is nothing grammatically wrong with the passive voice, but, when students use it, the effect is often to create vagueness because the passive voice tends to conceal or deflect agency. "Mathilda hit George with a hammer" becomes "George was hit with a hammer by Mathilda" or even worse (since the agency is concealed completely) "George was hit with a hammer."

Just look at these sentences in statistical terms. In the active voice version, there are six words and four of them are strong. (Remember William Hazlitt's dictum, "Every word must be a blow.") Only the preposition and the article fail to deliver a punch (and they never do). In the first passive voice version, there are eight words and only four of them carry a punch. We have suffered a statistically measurable dilution of linguistic force. Not only that, but we have to wait till the last word of the sentence before we have any idea what happened. In the third example, the second passive voice example, we are back to six words, but only three of them are strong words and we have an incomplete picture of the action in question. Mathilda has fallen out of the picture. No one is holding the hammer.

Look at your sentences and count the number of words with force and the number of words that are taking up space.

You can express the results as a percentage. In the above examples, the percentages are 66%, 50% and 50%. The higher the percentage of words of force, the better the writing. You can always rewrite a sentence to change the ratio of words of force to place-taking words and improve the quality of the prose.

But a simple percentage like this doesn't tell the whole story. The best of the three sentences I've just been discussing is "Mathilda hit George with the hammer." We've been mulling it over for less than a couple of minutes and already it's getting boring. The key to the boredom is the generic quality of the diction, words like the verb "hit" and the noun "hammer." And this is a problem I find in student writing over and over again. Student writers are often satisfied with what I call "sketching in" an action. They leave it to the reader to supply the precise details.

I count words. Students obviously don't, otherwise they would notice how they lean on generic action verbs like "look," "see," "sit," "stand," "move," "turn," and "walk." I find page after page of student work in which there is not one spritely, interesting action described. Often the same dull verb is used again and again. When I point this out, often it has no effect—because changing the verb would mean work, the work of actually imagining precisely what the scene, characters and action in question really look like and communicating that to the reader. In this sense, many student stories are little more than notes toward a story. So how about: "Mathilda smashed George in the head with his own ball-pean hammer, making a sound like a slap" (59% words of force) or "Mathilda tagged George on the head with Uncle Zuba's prized antique claw-hammer, just enough to make him noddy but not kill him"? (64%) In both these examples not only have I increased the power, precision and number of the verbs, but I have also added narrative and descriptive elements as well as moments of irony and dramatic contrast. In the second example, as I begin to warm to the task, I find the words "tagged" and "noddy" which are beginning to get twisty and odd in a pleasant and exciting way. Rewriting tired, generic, flaccid prose gives you the opportunity to do this.

F. Scott Fitzgerald wrote (in a letter to his daughter Scottie—lucky girl): "All fine prose is based on the verbs carrying the sentences. Probably the finest technical poem in English is Keats' 'Eve of St. Agnes.' A line like 'The hare limped trembling through the frozen grass,' is so alive that you race through it, scarcely noticing it, yet it has colored the whole poem with its movement—the limping, trembling and freezing is going on before your own eyes." When we read good narrative prose, we discover over and over that this is true.

Here is an example from a memoir, *As I Walked Out One Midsummer Morning*, by the English poet Laurie Lee. In a passage picked at random—not his full-out best writing, just a workmanlike, getting-the-job-done passage of fine prose—he writes:

> The country east of Tarifa *was* high, bare, and brown as a mangy lion, with kites and vultures *turning* slowly overhead, *square-winged*, like electric fans. It *was* a *scrub-covered* wilderness, *rippling* with wind, but heartless, empty of life, except for occasional hunters who *appeared* suddenly with muskets, *fired* at nothing, then *went* away.

Two sentences, fifty-three words. A description of a Spanish landscape. The two main predicate verbs are "to be," but the passage is alive with precise, concrete actions: "turning," "square-winged," "scrub-covered," "rippling," "appeared," "fired," "went away." In two sentences (aside from all the other rhetorical activity going on), there are nine verbs or verb-constructions. Lee's landscape is seething with life. Here is what he does when he has a character in the scene:

> Suddenly he *turned* to the young fisherman, *handed* him a carton of cigarettes, and *spoke* to him in a rapid *whisper*.

The fisherman *listened, spat, shrugged* his shoulders, then *got up* and *went* to the door. He *whistled* twice, and from the shadow of an *upturned* boat another shadow *detached* itself. The Cuban *left* the half-bottle of whisky behind him and *went* to the *waiting* girl on the beach.

Four sentences, seventy words, fifteen verbs, verbal adjectives, or verb-nouns: "turned," "handed," "spoke," "whisper," "listened," "spat," "shrugged," "got up," "went," "whistled," "upturned," "detached," "left," "went," "waiting." (I count the word "whisper" which is actually a noun but is so close to being a verb in context.) Some of the verbs have that generic quality I mentioned earlier, but Lee packs in so much action in quick bursts that we don't have to dwell on them. Often the generic verbs are capped with a stronger more precise action—"turned," "handed," and "spoke" go on to "whisper"; "listened" goes on to "spat" and "shrugged" (a lovely triplet). And Lee renders a rhetorical climax of that beautiful verb "detached" and the action of one shadow detaching itself weirdly from another shadow (the word "shadow" repeated) in the night. Also notice the lovely little inversion that makes a bit of poetry at the end. Instead of "the girl waiting on the beach" the Cuban goes to meet the "waiting girl on the beach."

Here's a passage from Elizabeth Bowen's novel *The Death of the Heart*, the opening paragraph:

That morning's ice, no more than a brittle film, *had cracked* and *was* now *floating* in segments. These *tapped* together or, *parting, left* channels of dark water, down which swans in slow indignation *swam*. The islands *stood* in *frozen* woody brown dusk: it *was* now between three and four in the afternoon. A sort of *breath* from the clay, from the city outside the park, *condensing, made* the air unclear; through this, the trees around the lake *soared* frigidly up. Bronze cold of January *bound* the sky and the landscape; the sky *was shut* to the sun—but the swans, the rims of ice, the pallid *withdrawn* Regency terraces *had* an unnatural *burnish*, as though cold *were* light. There *is* something momentous about the height of winter. *Steps rang* on the bridges, and along the black *walks*. This weather *had set* in; it would *freeze* harder tonight.

This is a landscape opening that also tells the reader where and when the novel starts and what the weather is like which, in turn, establishes a certain atmosphere. But as with Lee's landscapes this one is astir with life and movement. How is it done? Well, there are eight sentences, one hundred and forty seven words and twenty-three verbs, verbal adjectives or verbal nouns: "cracked," "floating," "tapped," "parting," "left," "swam," "was," "breath," "condensing," "made," "soared," "bound," "was shut," "withdrawn," "had," "burnish," "were," "is," "steps," "rang," "walks," "set in," "freeze." (Note the one deft instance of the passive voice.) You can express this again as a ratio: in this passage, Bowen writes a 23/8 verb-to-sentence ratio, three verbs per sentence. In the two Laurie Lee passages, the ratio is 7/2 and 15/4, almost four verbs per sentence. Again, simple ratios don't tell nearly the whole rhetorical story, but they begin to tell you about verbs. Beyond the ratio you should immediately notice the quality of the verbs: three copulas ("was," "is," "were"), one passive voice ("was shut"), three generics ("left," "had," "made") and one slightly abstract verb ("set in") against fifteen precise, concrete actions.

We can be sure that Bowen knows exactly what she is doing because she has written about her writing practice. In this case, she is discussing an early scene in her novel *The House in Paris*, and she is talking specifically about how to make a static scene come alive. First a paragraph from the text in question:

Mme. Fisher's bedroom, though it *was* over the salon, had two windows, not one. Jalousies *were pulled* to over the far window, so that no light *fell* across the head of the bed. A cone of sick-room incense on the bureau *sent spirals up* the daylight near the door; daylight *fell* cold white on the honeycomb quilt *rolled back*. Round the *curtained* bed-head, Pompeian red walls *drank* objects into their shadow: picture frames, armies of bottles, boxes, an ornate clock *showed* without *glinting*, as though not quite *painted out* by some transparent *wash*. Henrietta *had never been* in a room so full and still. She *stood* by the door Miss Fisher *had shut* behind her, with her heart in her mouth. Her eyes *turned* despairingly to a bracket on which *stood spiked* shells with cameos on their lips. The airlessness *had* a strange dry pure physical smell.

Quantitative analysis: one hundred and forty-seven words, eight sentences, eighteen verbs or verbal adjectives and nouns: "was," "were pulled," "fell," "sent spirals up," "fell," "rolled back," "drank," "showed," "glinting," "pointed out," "wash," "had never been," "stood," "had shut," "turned," "stood," "spiked," "had." One in eight words is a verb of some form. Qualitative analysis: three copulas ("was," "were," "had never been"), one passive voice verb ("were pulled"), seven generic or relatively inactive verbs ("showed," "stood," "shut," "stood," "turned," "stood," "had"), and ten concrete action verbs, ("fell," "sent spirals up," "fell," "rolled back," "curtained," "drank," "glinting," "painted out," "wash," "spiked"). It's interesting to note that, when Bowen uses a weaker verb, she often supports it with either another stronger word or an adverb. For example, the weaker verb "stood" is juxtaposed with the strong verbal adjective "spiked" and the two words are linked by alliteration; they become one strong verbal idea. When she uses the weaker verb "turn," she adds the adverb "despairingly" to render the movement more concrete and particular. The passive voice here is correctly used to describe an act already completed by an unknown hand; we see the result of the action, but we do not know the agent.

Here is what Bowen says about this text. Note, curiously enough, she shows evidence of suffering from my word-counting mania.

> Yet this passage makes contradictory use of four vigorous anti-static verbs: "sent spirals up," "fell," "drank," "turned." It brings into the picture three (anti-static) lately completed acts: jalousies pulled to, quilt rolled back, door shut behind Henrietta. Further, there is an evocation of action thwarted (or withheld energy): light (because of the jalousies) does *not* fall across the head of the bed; ornate clock, glassy bottles, etc., show but "without glinting"; . . . The one thing in action here is the incense cone consuming itself by its slow burning (and *it* is a sickness symbol). (*Pictures and Conversations*)

Here is a passage by an American writer who early caught my attention for the vigor and energy of his prose—Leonard Michaels. The story is called "City Boy"—the opening lines, almost hysterical with the proliferation of verbs:

> "Phillip," she *said*, "this is crazy."
>
> I *didn't agree* or *disagree*. She *wanted* some answer. I *bit* her neck. She *kissed* my ear. It *was* nearly three in the morning. We had just *returned*. The apartment *was* dark and quiet. We *were* on the *living* room floor and she *repeated*, "Phillip, this is crazy." Her crinoline *broke* under us like cinders. Furniture *loomed* all around—settee, chairs, a table with a lamp. Pictures *were* cloudy blotches *drifting* above. But no lights, no things to *look* at, no eyes in her

head. She *was* underneath me and warm. The rug *was* warm, soft as mud, deep. Her crinoline *cracked* like sticks. Our naked bellies *clapped* together. Air *fired* out like farts. I *took* it as applause. The chandelier *clicked*. The clock *ticked* as if to *split* its glass.

Twenty-one sentences, one hundred and thirty-six words, twenty-four verbs, not counting the noun phrase and the action nouns: "said," "didn't agree," "[didn't] disagree", "wanted," "bit," "kissed," "was," "had returned," "was," "were," "repeated," "broke," "loomed," "were drifting," "to look," "was," "was," "cracked," "clapped," "fired," "took," "clicked," "ticked," "to split." The verb-to-sentence ratio (not counting the verbs in dialogue) is 1/1, apparently low, but this doesn't take into account the brevity of the sentences and absence of subordination. The verb-to-total word count ratio is 24/136, one word in six is a verb. And a qualitative analysis reads like this: five copulas ("was," "was," "were," "was," "was"), two speech attributions ("said," "repeated"), and seventeen strong, active verbs. In one sentence, the verb is elided, the copula is implied but left out (a good tactic when used occasionally).

Finally, a counter-example, lest I be accused of stacking the deck by only picking writers who write the way I want them to write. Virginia Woolf is one of those writers who suffers most in our post-literate age, being held up as an example of anti-male, dreamy, interior, stream of consciousness prose with very little action. Post-literate readers and writers think there is much virtue in oblique, quiet, little, domestic stories because these are the sorts of stories Virginia Woolf is supposed to have written. Post-literate readers get this impression from the air; more often than not they haven't read her, and if they have read her, they don't read carefully enough to notice what she is really doing on the page, being guided and blinded by their own preconceptions. Post-literate readers and writers don't know the difference between good and bad writing, can't even see it on the page. (But don't get me started.)

Here is a passage from *Jacob's Room*. Once again I choose, almost at random, not an especially flowery or dramatic moment, not the full authorial orchestra, but an example of the author's standard, work-a-day good writing, the stuff good and great novels are made of.

> The little boys in the front bedroom *had thrown* off their blankets and *lay* under the sheets. It *was* hot; rather sticky and steamy. Archer *lay spread out*, with one arm *striking* across the pillow. He *was flushed*; and when the heavy curtain *blew* out a little he *turned* and *half opened* his eyes. The wind actually *stirred* the cloth on the chest of drawers, and *let in* a little light, so that the sharp edge of the chest of drawers *was* visible, *running* straight up, until a white shape *bulged out*; and a silver streak *showed* in the *looking-glass*.

Here we have ninety-nine words, five sentences, eighteen verbs or verbal adjectives or verbal nouns (I'm counting "looking-glass"—she could written "mirror"). More than three verbs per sentence. Almost one in five words is a verb. And the qualitative analysis gives this result: three copulas ("was," "was [flushed]," "was [visible]"), four more or less generic verbs ("lay," "lay," "turned," "let in"), a couple of borderline generic verbs ("showed" and "looking"), and six concrete, specific, and even violent action verbs ("spread out," "striking," "blew," "stirred," "running," "bulged"). Note that Woolf's characteristically impressionistic visual effect comes not from any vagueness of language but from a very precise delineation of angle of view (half-opened eyes, reflected in the mirror), lighting (a little light when the breeze blows the curtain open), and shape (sharp edge, white shape, silver streak) which makes what she is describing seem more like an abstract painting than a piece of furniture. And all these elements—point of view, light and shape—are in motion, even violently so. Take out the verbs and the passage is dead.

Here's one other bit from the same novel. She's describing Jacob reading Plato, aside from sleeping, possibly the most passively ruminative and inactive pastime one could think of putting in a book.

> The *Phaedrus is* very difficult. And so, when at length one *reads* straight ahead, *falling* into step, *marching* on, *becoming* (so it *seems*) momentarily part of this *rolling*, imperturbable energy, which *has driven* darkness before it since Plato *walked* the Acropolis, it *is* impossible to *see* to the fire.
>
> The *dialogue draws* to a *close*. Plato's *argument is* done. Plato's *argument is stowed* away in Jacob's mind, and for five minutes Jacob's mind *continues* alone, onwards, into the darkness. Then, *getting up*, he *parted* the curtains, and *saw*, with astonishing clearness, how the Springetts opposite *had gone* to bed; how it *rained*; how the Jews and the foreign woman, at the end of the street, *stood* by the pillar-box, *arguing*.

One hundred and twenty words, six sentences, twenty-two verbs ("is," "reads," "falling in step," "marching," "becoming," "seems," "rolling," "has driven," "walked," "is," "see," "draws," "is," "is stowed," "continues," "getting up," "parted," "saw," "had gone to bed," "rained," "stood," "arguing"). And this is not counting action nouns like "dialogue" and "argument." More than one in six words is a verb, nearly four verbs per sentence (due to deft subordination and Woolf's use of participles). Note the use of two verbs that are military metaphors (does this surprise readers with preconceived notions of how Woolf writes?)

and the way the passage ends with the participle "arguing" which echoes the two iterations of the word "argument" at the commencement of the paragraph and renders the action at the end of the scene as ongoing and continuous.

Good prose is vigorous, aboil with verbs, packed with motion and conflict and story at the level of sentences themselves. Post-literate readers and writers do not notice this, and, when they come to write, cannot replicate the sheer imaginative density of concrete, precise action that is necessary to make words come alive on the page. When they read, they assemble a story summary in their heads, rather than make the effort to study the words on the page; when they write, they make sketches of stories, thin and vague, barely the ghosts of stories.

THE DRAMA
OF GRAMMAR

THE FIRST PROBLEM of style is how to make dead things come alive. By dead things, I mean words, which neither move, nor breathe, nor weep, nor lust, nor love. Writing well means raising the dead. It means making the dead words dance. In the previous essay I discussed the way we can use verbs to make a Lazarus out of a dying sentence. And I have waxed belligerent on the minimal requirement of grammatical clarity for the production of good prose. Now I'll talk about the use of contrast and antithesis and what I call "but-constructions" to create drama at the level of sentences and paragraphs.

The term "but-construction" is my own coinage, of course. Somewhat facetious. I define a but-construction as any use of the conjunction "but" or synonym, also any functionally similar punctuation marks including line-breaks, in a sentence or a paragraph to set up an antithesis, surprise, reversal, contrast, paradox, or comparison. The beauty of a but-construction is that it creates conflict at the level of sentences; it creates drama out of a grammatical occasion, and by "drama" here I mean not character action, that is, our present-day version of the ritualistic "things done" which is the meaning of the original Greek term, but mental drama, the clash of ideas, motives, expectations and outcomes. It is the mental drama, the element of surprise and mystery implicit in the plot of every sentence we write, that contributes to the feeling that a piece of prose is alive, and further contributes to that density of action, interest and delight which we expect from good writing.

It seems a simple thing. In some ways, it's almost too simple to notice. And I certainly spent years, bumbling creature that I am, trying to figure out how to write interesting sentences before stumbling on the obvious. I studied grammar texts, composition manuals, and encyclopedias of rhetoric. I tried to write those topic-sentence paragraphs they teach you in high school. I composed balanced sentences and periodic sentences and practiced, till I was blue in the face, the English department adage, Vary your sentence structure. Amazingly enough, having a mix of long and short sentences, along with topic-body-conclusion paragraph structure, did not automatically make my prose interesting. Rather, the trend was in the opposite direction. And to be sure, like most beginning writers, I was sometimes using the word "but" in sentences without being conscious of its diverse utility.

But one day I was reading Alice Munro, trying to figure out what she was doing to make her prose memorable. I happened to read this paragraph in her story "Lives of Girls and Women" (from the book of the same title which is sometimes called a novel) when I began to see the light, the way, the mystic tao.

> "Don't get vicious," said Fern. "I mean it." Her voice was small for such a big woman, plaintive, put-upon, but in the end good-humoured, yielding. All those qualities my mother had developed for her assault upon life—sharpness, smartness, determination, selectiveness—seemed to have their opposites in Fern, with her diffuse complaints, lazy movements, indifferent agreeableness. She had a

dark skin, not olive but dusty looking, dim, with brown pigmented spots as large as coins; it was like the dappled ground under a tree on a sunny day. Her teeth were square, white, slightly protruding, with little spaces between them. These two characteristics, neither of which sounds particularly attractive in itself, did give her a roguish, sensual look.

Superficially, this is a run-of-the-mill descriptive passage, telling us what the new character Fern looks like. This is the kind of passage I used to dread writing myself and still dread reading in student work because everyone feels he has to do it and it mostly comes out boring. What makes this passage interesting? Well, to begin with, it's built on contrasts; all Munro's assertions are couched as conflicted juxtapositions. A student would start by writing, "Fern was a big woman." Munro writes that her voice was small for a big woman. Then comes the "but"; the voice is small, plaintive and put-upon, but with the "but" the sentence veers back on itself, cancelling the steady accretion of negative epithets, reversing the flow of meaning with a dramatic abruptness.

In the following sentence ("All those qualities . . ."), Munro does one of her classic moves—Munro hardly ever leaves a character standing by herself in a paragraph. To describe Fern, she tells us first about the narrator's mother and then the "opposite" traits in Fern. We get two lists of characteristics, diametrically opposed.

The next sentence ("She had a dark skin . . .") contains a second but-construction, or a version of it, the not-but-construction. And here you have to imagine the sentence without the interruption. "She had a dark skin . . . with brown pigmented spots as large as coins . . ." It's not bad, mind you, with the nice simile at the end. But when you look at the sentence Munro actually wrote you can clearly see the excitement, the mental hurly-burly, created by the but-construction. "She had a dark skin, not olive but dusty looking, dim, with brown pigmented spots as large as coins . . ." At some level of consciousness, not to be determined by you and me, Munro has realized that the adjective "dark" is dull and needs support. She adds the quasi-parenthetical not-but-construction to interrupt the normal flow of the sentence, the expected rhythm. She supports and modifies the adjective "dark" by juxtaposing the words "olive" and "dusty" in a gorgeous and grammatically exciting fight. The sentence becomes a cockpit, the reading mind has to do a little work, rhythms are altered.

The clause following the semicolon and the next complete sentence are the only straightforward subject-predicate clauses in the paragraph (albeit the principle of contrast is still at work—the whiteness of Fern's teeth is clearly designed as a contrast with her dark skin). And they set up the last sentence which caps the three-sentence sequence at the end of the paragraph. This last sentence, too, is straightforward, or begins that way. But Munro, just as she did earlier, inserts a quasi-parenthetical fight. Read the sentence without the interruption: "These two characteristics . . . did give her a roguish, sensual look." Perfectly all right, nothing wrong with it. But then add the jazz: "These two characteristics, neither of which sounds particularly attractive in itself, did give her a roguish, sensual look." The fight this time is between the two "unattractive" traits—dark skin, protruding teeth—and the final "roguish, sensual look."

Munro constructs Fern's appearance in a series of sentences that build on contrasts, oppositions, and abrupt reversals of energy and value. Bad traits turn into good traits at the word "but." (I make an argument to myself that the last sentence in the passage under analysis is really a tacit but-construction.) Fern and the narrator's mother are opposites. The rhythm of standard English sentence structure is insistently interrupted with quasiparentheticals and but-constructions which present new oppositions and alternatives.

If you mentally chart the energy flow, the beat of meaning and value, as it jumps from word to word, instead of a standard English subject-verb-predicate, you get these zigzag shapes like a skier going down a slalom course, and each turn presents a surprising twist in meaning, a contrary assertion, a denial, and transformation. This is action, drama and conflict at the level of sentences, in the grammar, as it were, of the clauses, sentences and paragraphs. The underlying principle has something to do with juxtaposition and opposition, with contrast and surprise. The specific grammatical form that expresses the principle is the but-construction.

A few lines later in the same story we find a paragraph that begins "Fern Dogherty and my mother were friends in spite of differences." I won't give you the whole long paragraph, but as we get to the three-quarter mark we find these sentences:

> My mother had a book of operas. She would get it out and follow the story, identifying the arias, for which translations were provided. She had questions for Fern, but Fern did not know as much about opera as you would think she might; she would even get mixed up about which one it was they were listening to. But sometimes she would lean forward with her elbows on the table, not now relaxed, but alertly supported, and sing, scorning the foreign words.

Once again, this is a paragraph that describes a character by contrasting two characters. But the sentences at the emotional and syntactic core of the paragraph exhibit a flurry of "buts"; in one sentence there are two occurrences. And the zigzag pattern is clear. The first "but," a conjunction joining two principle clauses, extends the contrast between the mother and Fern and introduces the information that Fern doesn't really know as much about music as someone who once trained for the opera should. In other words, she's a bit dim. But the following sentence ("But sometimes she would . . ."), with the two "buts," reverses the negative trend with the beautiful image of the suddenly alert and singing Fern. The mother has a book, an intellect, and questions, but poor, dim Fern can enter the music with her heart.

The structure of the clause in question is fascinating. The sentence begins with a "but," which is against everything my school-boy training taught me. But the whole paragraph turns on this "but," which, as I say, reverses the flow of energy and brings Fern a species of grace. The second "but" comes near the end of the principle clause, which in itself is unexceptional grammatically, a straightforward subject-verb-predicate clause. And this is another of Munro's not-but-constructions ("not now relaxed, but alertly supported"); it's a fight between the image of a dim, relaxed, unaware Fern and the Fern infected by the music, now alert.

The paragraph, taken as a whole, is a struggle for Fern's soul. Are we to see only her dumpiness, her dimness, her ineffectual side, the Fern the townspeople laugh at and gossip about, the failed provincial opera singer? Or will we see her as a human being with a heart, with a potential for beauty that somehow redeems her? In effect, the paragraph has conflict and plot. But the conflict and plot are essentially grammatical in provenance.

What did I make of this? Literary bumbler and humble seeker that I am? With my mix of long and short sentences with the occasional periodic something-or-other thrown in? The lesson I took from reading Munro was that the injunction to vary sentence structure was beside the point because you could vary sentence structure endlessly and the prose would still be dead unless you could infuse it with some sort of cerebral action. The sentences themselves needed plot, conflict, action. This is akin to the difference between the narrator's mother with her intellectual understanding of music and Fern who understands music from the inside. The structure of the sentences can be varied by rote, from the outside as it were, or they can be written from the inside in the spirit of conflict and life. If you write that way, splicing contrasting elements together, creating a fight, adding subordinate elements that increase tension, interrupt the expected grammatical logic of your clauses, delay the resolution of the syntax, and then finally resolve it; the sentences will be varied in a beautiful and exciting way.

The great Scottish writer Robert Louis Stevenson is now remembered mostly for his boys' adventure books *Kidnapped* and *Treasure Island* and that little masterpiece of Gothic horror *Dr. Jekyll and Mr. Hyde*, which, if mostly unread in these post-literate days, remains iconic like Mary Shelley's *Frankenstein*. Stevenson also wrote a marvellous and forgotten essay called "On Some Technical Elements of Style in Literature" in which he says:

> Communication may be made in broken words; the business of life carried on in substantives alone; but that is not what we call literature; and the true business of the literary artist is to plait or weave his meaning, involving it around itself so that each sentence, by successive phrases, shall first come into a kind of knot, and then, after a moment of suspended meaning, solve and clear itself.

This is a gorgeous sentence, one of the touchstones of my self-training. We note that it turns on the word "but" and a contrast between mere communication as against literary writing. At the beginning, there is a fight. But the sentence is basically a compound, and after the conjunction "and" it goes on to describe the literary art of composition. If you read the sentence carefully out loud you can feel in the rhythm of the phrasing that the sound, form, and rhythm of the words exactly replicates the meaning of the words, so that when Stevenson reaches the word "knot" he has also reached the apex, the peak, the precise knotting of syntax, rhythm, and thought that he has described. What follows is a pause and a resolution, the quiet diminuendo and conclusion of the period. The pattern is fight, rising action, knot, suspension and resolution.

A bit later he describes in more detail how to construct literary sentences—note again how the pattern of the sentence repeats the pattern of the thought.

> Style is synthetic; and the artist, seeking, so to speak, a peg to plait about, takes up at once two or more elements or two or more views of the subject at hand; combines, implicates and contrasts them; and while, in one sense, he is merely seeking an occasion for the necessary knot, he will be found, in the other, to have greatly enriched the meaning, or to have transacted the work of two sentences in the space of one.

The pattern of this sentence inverts the pattern of the previous example; the fight, so to speak, is near the end, and it's a quieter little fight. The sentence begins with an assertion and then a discussion of method, runs a triplet of verbs, a sudden machine-gun rhythm, and then there is a quasi-parenthetical interruption couched as a subordinate clause ("and while, in one sense . . ."), much like the not-but phrases Munro uses in her sentences. Here Stevenson contrasts the idea that the writer is following the form for form's sake, merely to set up "the necessary knot," with the idea that the meaning of the sentence, of the thought itself, has been amplified, that is, new content has been created in satisfying the demand of form. Read the sentence aloud and the word "knot" corresponds with the peak of intensity. It's followed by a couple of suspending phrases, and then the sentence resolves itself. The resolution of the fight is not that one alternative is true, but both.

There are several things to notice here. First of all, the pattern of Stevenson's sentences is similar to the pattern of Munro's sentences and paragraphs. The differences are not essential. Munro is writing fiction and she is a contemporary; her language is less formally constrained. Stevenson is writing non-fiction, an argument, and he wrote when you could still pepper the page with semicolons and it looked all right. Munro uses the semicolons, too, just not as many. Her periods are nevertheless a bit briefer than his. But they both compose rhythmically; they both know how to vary the rhythm with a run, a triplet, or with an interruptive parenthetical, and they both know how to construct around a contrast, reach a climax and a turn.

Stevenson says style is synthetic. When I first began to read Munro, her style seemed so relaxed, so natural I couldn't see it. It seemed the antithesis of Stevenson's synthetic, artificially constructed prose. I use the word "artificially" on purpose here. Stevenson's sentences do seem the slightest bit artificial, but I suspect that's because he is showing off or his rhythms are ever so slightly antique. When you examine Munro's sentences carefully they seem just as artificial, artfully constructed around a contrast and those but-constructions. Mere communication doesn't require her to combine so artfully the mother and Fern in those paragraphs: a bullet point list would do just as well.

This artificiality of structure is evidence of form, that is, structure that goes beyond simple grammatical correctness to complicate and impede communication (content) in an aesthetically pleasing way. What fascinates me about form is that once you understand it, it becomes a blank space to be filled with content; we're so used to thinking of content as primary to form that, at first, this seems like a strange idea. This particular form or congeries of forms—the doubling or contrast of juxtaposition, the fight of contrast, the expectation and denial of expectation, the interruption, the but-construction—demands content that might not initially be there for the sake of completeness. It is an "occasion," as Stevenson calls it, for verbal excitement. In a sense, form implies, requires, or even creates content.

The easiest way to see what I mean is to imagine any simple declarative sentence and add the word "but" to the end. "The barn was red" is a simple communication and a grammatically correct utterance. But is it beautiful, exciting or even interesting? "The barn was red, but . . ." implies complexity and story. It says things are not as simple as you thought they were. "The barn was red in the setting sun, but the boards, upon closer examination, were faded except for flecks of old paint, and there were stars of splintered wood where the bullets had gone in, and the hired man's body slumped abandoned against the foundation where he had fallen." Now this is just a riff, a little nothing, but it possesses a story. I wrote the word "but" and then had to write something else; the blank space demands completeness. I had no idea what I might put in there before I wrote the words. The result is pure invention, discovery, and rather fun. And this is the difference between mere communication and writing stories or essays or poems. In writing stories there is always the element of excitement and discovery implied in the demand of form.[1]

Here is one of my favourite poems: "They Flee From Me" by Thomas Wyatt.

> They fle from me that sometyme did me seke
> With naked fote stalking in my chamber.
> I have seen them gentill tame and meke
> That nowe are wyld and do not remembre
> That sometyme they put thimself in daunger
> To take bred at my hand; and nowe they raunge

Besely seking with a continuell chaunge.
Thancked be fortune, it hath ben othrewise
Twenty tymes better; but ons in speciall,
In thyn arraye after a pleasaunt gyse,
When her lose gowne from her shoulders did fall,
And she me caught in her armes long and small;
Therewithall swetely did me kysse,
And softely saide, dere hert, howe like you this?

It was no dreme: I lay brode awaking.
But all is torn thorough my gentilnes
Into a straunge fasshion of foresaking;
And I have leve to goo of her goodnes,
And she also to use new fangilnes.
But syns that I so kyndely ame served,
I fain would knowe what she hath deserved.

I could go on and on about the felicities of this poem, but I want mainly to look at the details of structure that are not strictly poetical but in keeping with my discussion so far. Once again we see the now-familiar zigzag pattern, the line and sentence structure built on a series of contrasts. The two basic contrasts are "then" against "now," and between the women who loved the poet and the fickle women who flee from him now that he's getting old ("seek" and "flee" in the first line; doesn't it remind you of "big" and "small" in Alice Munro's sentence?). But the third stanza also begins with an abrupt contrast between dreaming and sleeping. Also in the third stanza, which turns on a "but," we see the poet's mood changing from bemused melancholy to sudden anger.

The zigzag of value vectors alter direction sometimes at the line break, sometimes inside the line, and sometimes at the stanza break. And there are three but-constructions. The first comes in the second stanza and signals an abrupt change from the general to the particular, a sudden move into scene and even dialogue which nails, for the poet, the moment when love and beauty belonged to him. The third stanza contains two "buts." The first wakes the poet up from his love-reverie into the cold present and the strange fashion of forsaking. The second signals his turn into anger that brings the poem to a close.

Again, mere communication does not require this much contrivance; the poetic machinery is somehow gratuitous, surplus. Imagine a fictional student writer, the one who wrote "The barn was red" and thought it sufficient. Imagine if Alice Munro had written: "Fern Dogherty was fat, dim, dark-skinned and didn't know much about music." Imagine our student expressing Thomas Wyatt's poetic intention in an email: "I'm upset because I'm getting old and those fickle girls don't find me attractive any more." I ask myself, What gets lost in mere communication? Some almost sensual but mainly cerebral pleasure, perhaps, in the sheer motion of the beats of value.

Nabokov says somewhere that we read with our spines, by which I take it that he meant there is a physical component to our imaginative interaction with a text. Sometimes, when I'm writing, I imagine that I am standing behind the reader holding his head in my hands as his eyes follow the words, moving it this way and that and up and down and sometimes slapping him a couple of times to surprise him—he seems to like it, poor masochistic bugger. To return to my skiing metaphor: the difference between mere communication and Wyatt's poem or a paragraph by Alice Munro is the difference between standing on your skis in a flat field and zipping down a slalom course at very high speed. The mind takes pleasure in motion, it takes joy in syntactical disturbances, it becomes somehow more itself in the drama of grammar.

In his lovely book on evolutionary psychology, *Origins of the Modern Mind*, Merlin Donald traces the development of mental machines that as an organized aggregate form the symbol-generating and reading super-machine we call the literate mind. These machines include various short and long-term memory storage devices, image-generating devices, feedback systems, etc. In order to read an Alice Munro sentence or a Thomas Wyatt poem, the mind has to bring a number of these machines and storage devices into play simultaneously. To understand a contrasting juxtaposition or a but-construction requires among other things that we simultaneously suspend before the mind the contrasting items and their attributes long enough to make sense of the sentence or paragraph or poem.

What I describe earlier as a "fight" inside the sentence is precisely this simultaneous juggling or balancing of contraries or opposites for the time it takes to finish the sentence, the suspension of syntactic elements in the mind creating suspense, the mind waiting to see how things turn out. It's pleasant to speculate, following Donald, that the contrasting bits of meaning are remembered in different parts of the brain so that the palpable zigzag feeling you get reading these passages is in fact the result of some sort of electronic backing and forthing going on inside the skull. Why that might be pleasurable instead of disturbing, I don't know. And when the grammar is wonky and the sentences don't complete themselves appropriately, it is disturbing, disorienting—the cerebral equivalent of motion sickness.

I am feeling my way toward a general principle here, something like the idea that good prose is not a straight line to the truth but a zigzag path involving the juxtaposition of opposites or contraries, the denial of expectation and but-constructions, that literary writing reveals a truth that is surplus to the truth of a mere message and that this truth has something to do with the placement of words, their syntactic ordering, and that good sentences are an adventure not a plod. Note how much beauty and energy derives in these examples from the simple doubling of terms; that is, the energy derives from putting two contrasting items in a sentence instead of making a simple statement of fact (Fern and the narrator's mother, communication and literary prose, Wyatt's then and now).

Now think for a moment about aphorisms, short, pithy statements which often use balanced construction and antithesis. Historically they are related to the Greek poetic form the epigram which was a short poem, meant to be memorable, often an epitaph (and therefore sometimes cut in stone, hence the word "lapidary" used to describe this sort of rhetorical style). Aphorisms are synthetic, artificially constructed, highly formal little sayings. The first we know of were written by Hippocrates in a book called, yes, *Aphorisms*. For example, "Life is short, art is long, opportunity fleeting, experimenting dangerous, reasoning difficult." Notice the balanced antithesis, short and long, which reminds us once more of Alice Munro and Stevenson and Wyatt. Notice also the succeeding elements, the juxtaposed nouns and modifiers with the verbs elided, which is, I gather, typical of certain Greek poetic forms. The effect is terse, startling, almost iconic.

There are many forms of aphorisms, or constructions that look pretty much like aphorisms. "Life is a dream; when we sleep we are awake, and when awake we sleep." (Montaigne) They are very good for rendering thought vigorously, concisely and authoritatively in narrative or in essays. "Vision is exorcism." (Laurence Durrell) "All reformers are bachelors." (George Moore) "The man of action is always ruthless; no one has a conscience except an observer." (Goethe) They sound witty (and are related rhetorically to jokes). "That one had dreams of becoming a legend in his own time, but succeeded in becoming only a rumour." (The pseudonymous Hooper Thorne) Sometimes they are wise (and are related to the so-called wisdom literature of the ancients). "Love of justice in most men is no more than the fear of suffering injustice." (La Rochefoucauld) They are dramatic and provocative. "There are two positions available to us—either crime which renders us happy, or the noose, which prevents us from being unhappy." (de Sade)[2]

There are also extended aphorisms in which the two or more balanced contraries or opposites are batted back and forth for a paragraph or more. See Theodor Adorno's *Minima Moralia* for a modern example. Many of Nietszche's books are collections of aphorisms; recognizing their synthetic and thus experimental flavour, he called his fragments *versuch*, that is, they were trials or attempts or essays in the root sense of the word (from the French "to try or attempt"). In my novel *The Life and Times of Captain N.* there are a series of sections that come under the subhead "from Oskar's Book about Indians" which are extended aphorisms contrasting the white European culture of the book with Native American orality. Needless to say, this is not a structure I invented: I learned it studying the essayistic intercalations in Milan Kundera's novels.

What has always fascinated me about aphorisms is their mysterious combination of artificiality (Stevenson's synthetic quality) and their aura of authority and wisdom. The artificiality is always threatening to cancel the authority; aphorisms are ineffably paradoxical. They are a form of thought in which the form somehow precedes the content, which seems like putting the cart before the horse. The form of aphoristic thought is a fight, a juxtaposition of contrasts, a balanced antithesis, which the writer invokes to satisfy the formal demand. And this content, which at the outset was only invented to satisfy the form, somehow turns into a real thought, that is, aphorisms create a surplus that seems to go beyond the mere form and the mere content and the artificiality of both.

We can recall here how Plato dramatized his ideas as dialogues, as confrontations between personas presenting conflicting ideas. One can only speculate why Plato did this. Was it the influence of the Greek theatre or a holdover from the pre-literate days of oral discourse? Did it somehow seem natural to him that ideas would be hammered out in public, in the *agon* of public debate? And we can also think here of the Russian critic Mikhail Bakhtin's use of the term "dialogic" to describe Dostoevsky's narrative strategies and by extension the novel as a form, even language itself. All language is dialogic, he says; that is, language is made up of discourses in competition, in a fight (in dialogue) with one another.

To some, it may seem counterintuitive, if not downright surprising, that language and thought themselves manifest this confrontational aspect, even more so that great writing draws its energy from battle. But, conversely, we begin to appreciate that the zigzag devices of doubling, contrasting, denial of expectation, Stevenson's knot, aphorisms, the poetic turn, the syntactic fights, antitheses, and but-constructions, seem less and less strange and more like a natural use of language, or in some way reflecting the nature of language and thought itself, less of a playful, and hence unnecessary elaboration, than a limb, an arm or a leg, which, if we choose to ignore it, leaves us limping along as half-writers, half-artists, half-thinkers.

Often when I am teaching, I find myself exhorting students to get more action on the page, and the students, bless their hearts, tend to think I want sex or a fistfight instead of the quiet little scene they have written. Often I don't mean that at all. What I mean is that their scene is missing the requisite density of syntactic action, the clash of values, the juxtaposition of contrasting elements, the raising of expectations and denial of same that make a sentence or a paragraph or a book or an essay or a poem exciting to read. Student stories tend to read, as I have said before, like sketches, rough outlines of stories. Student writers seem to feel that they are having enough trouble getting their characters in and out of rooms and somehow finding an ending without actually paying attention to the way they are writing the story. They may have a story sketch, but sentence after sentence doesn't read like it belongs in a story; they are too flat and generic, interested mainly in communicating the general idea not the excitement of creation and the astonishing particularity of the artistic experience.

Great prose or poetry goes somewhere else—it represents more than the mere message, complex as the message might be, that the words render; it becomes iconic; it pictures something beyond its mere aboutness, say, the room, the characters, the dialogue, the scene before us. The question to ask ourselves is, and here is the mystery: what is represented by the pleasurable organization of sentences and paragraphs that go to make up the work of art? What is represented by the syntactic confrontations and taut juxtapositions, the contrasts, the but-constructions, the rising plot and epilogue of literary sentences and paragraphs? What if the way literary communication takes place, the form of sentences, itself represents something? What is that something? Is it the nature of the human mind? Or the world? Or the nature of language as suggested by Bakhtin? Whole philosophies have attached themselves to one or another of these alternatives.

In her book-length essay *Economy of the Unlost*, which is about the Greek poet Simonides and the German poet Celan (a Munro-esque juxtaposition of similarity and contrast), Anne Carson writes that poetry can "render the invisible."

> Simonides seems to want to paint more than words seem to say. His iconic grammar renders a relationship that is mutual, dynamic and deeper than the visible surface of the language . . . When we consider Simonidean sentences, we see appearances engaged in a dialectic with one another, by participation of [the Greek *logos*, word] and [*icon*, picture] at once. We overhear a conversation that

sounds like reality. No other Greek writer of the period, except perhaps Heraklitos, uses the sentence in this way, as a "synthetic and tensional" unit that reenacts the reality of which it speaks. This is mimesis in its most radical mechanism.

I love that phrase "synthetic and tensional" because it can easily be applied to the sentence and paragraph structures I have been talking about in this essay. In these structures we see not a low-mimetic (to use Northrop Frye's term) representation of appearance but a dialectic of appearances, a clash, a fight, a conflict. In this aspect, of course, such structures resemble their literary cousins—irony, analogy and metaphor—wherein the reader's mind is also required, momentarily, to hold two or more ideas in tense opposition, such that what is portrayed is not the one or the other but the two in concert and thus some third evanescent and intangible article. This is the moment when beauty and excitement surpass utility in the play of language. The tantalizing possibility, as I have suggested, is that this clash itself is mimetic on a higher plane. Perhaps, like Simonides' sentences, the syntactic dramas of the but-construction, expectation and denial of same, doubling and contrast are an imitation of something. In terms of everyday reality, it would be a radical something, a something that eludes us wherever we look, mysterious and profound, like Quixote's Dulcinea, receding into the distance at every approach.

Notes

1. At a certain point, as I was teaching myself to be conscious of the but-construction, I realized how quick and useful the structure might be in introducing conflict into a story. The word "but" introduces conflict into a sentence; why not allow the story to develop from that jump-off point? So, if you read through my stories, you'll find a number of them that begin this way.

I thought my wife had left me, but she is back. What she has been doing the last two years I have no idea.

I am in bed with a woman who looks like a movie star, and I have lost my memory. (The "and" here functions as a tacit "but.")

The Indonesian client was due at 2:15 p.m., in exactly ten minutes according to my watch. But Bove, the CEO, had taken suddenly and mysteriously ill over lunch and had failed to return to the office.

This is how it goes: a boy named Iglaf, whose parents had immigrated from Estonia in the 1940s after much trouble in their native land, met a girl named Swan at a potluck supper and open mike reading in the basement of the Estonian Church on Broadview the summer of 1969. They became lovers that night, burnt a hole in his mattress with an overturned candle, drank wine from peanut butter jars and read their poems aloud between embraces. Near dawn they fell asleep in each other's arms, but then Swan woke up, wrapped a sheet around her breasts, sniffed the smell of burnt ticking in her hair, and stared at him. What was she trying to make out? What had disturbed her sleep?

The last example is instructive in a way that stands for them all. I wrote the opening lines and put the couple to sleep and then wrote the word "but" and all I could think of was that one of them woke up. So I wrote that, and then I was trying to figure out why she woke up because, obviously, somehow the story was there, and I couldn't think of anything. So I put down the rhetorical questions that corresponded to my own authorial reflections. In every one of these stories I had no idea what the story itself was about, where the grammatical trail would lead me. The "but" was a true jumping off point into the mystery of the white page. It created the demand for a certain kind of ongoing material, a demand for conflict, for a fight, for story.

2. Since every aphorist is an egomaniac, here is a selection of aphorisms culled from my own stories, novels, letters, and non-fiction.

Nostalgia is form; hope is content. (From "Dog Attempts to Drown Man in Saskatoon;" the syntax is modelled on the Hippocratic aphorism quoted above.)

Excessive obliquity leads straight to the Purgatory of vagueness. (From a letter to a student; the form involves the simple balanced contrast between "obliquity" and "vagueness.")

There are two kinds of readers—the adventurers who glory in the breathtaking audacity and risk of a well-turned aphorism and the weinies who, lacking courage themselves, find it an affront in others. (From a letter to a student; it's common to find an aphorism that starts, There are two kinds of x . . . , or, There are three kinds of x . . .)

This is what I think: the ways of God are not our ways; what are not our ways are the ways of God. (From my novel *Elle*: the form here is essentially a chiasmus, the criss-cross structure you find often in the Bible.)

The difference between pornography and literature is that in pornography everyone has orgasms all the time. There is no gap between desire and consummation. In literature there is always an element of frustration, displacement, delay and incompleteness (even if somebody does eventually manage to have an orgasm). (From *The Enamoured Knight*; again a common aphorism model begins with the words "The difference between . . ." and goes on to distinguish two contrary topics.)

THE MIND OF
ALICE MUNRO

ALICE MUNRO's constant concern is to correct the reader, to undercut and complicate her text until all easy answers are exhausted and an unnerving richness of life stands revealed in the particular, secret experiences of her characters. She does this in two ways. First, she has a sly capacity for filling her stories with sex, thwarted loves, betrayal and violence while self-presenting (somehow, in the prose) as a middle-aged Everywoman with only the faintest hint of a salacious gleam in her eye. And second, she deploys an amazing number of intricately interconnected literary devices that ironize and relativize meanings while conversely revealing (unveiling as in "apocalypse") an underground current of life that seems all the more true because it is hidden, earthy, frank, and shocking. In her story "Meneseteung," for example, the truth has something to do with menstruation, bloating, diarrhea and opium. That this truth is called into question at the story's close is pure Alice Munro, whose message may only be that life is never what you think it is.

"Meneseteung" advertises itself as *faux* amateur biography of a forgotten and forgettable "local" poet, a spinster named

Almeda Joynt Roth, who lived at the end of the 19th century in a small Ontario village just inside the advancing frontier. In 1879, Meda is drifting toward middle age when a salt well entrepreneur named Jarvis Poulter moves into town and half-heartedly begins to court her. One night Meda hears a drunken commotion in the street outside her house. Ignoring the ruckus, she manages to fall back asleep, but in the morning she discovers a woman's body in her backyard and runs to Jarvis's house, two doors down the street, for help. Jarvis nudges the body with his toe, pronounces the woman drunk and wipes his hand off on a leaf after shaking her roughly by the hair. Then, apparently aroused by Meda's nightgown (suddenly seeing her in a sexual light), he invites her to walk with him to church later in the morning (a decisive signal of interest in the world of the story). Meda is in a tizzy. She has taken a sleeping drug the evening before, her period is starting, she has diarrhea, she's making grape jelly; now she doses herself with nerve medicine (probably laudanum). Just before Jarvis shows up she pins a note to her front door; Jarvis retreats in silence. Meda spends the rest of the day in a drug haze, imagining the townspeople as gravestones toddling down the street. Then life returns to normal; only Jarvis is no longer interested in paying court to Meda. In 1903, village louts chase the eccentric old biddy into a nearby swamp. She catches cold and dies, leaving behind a slim volume of poems entitled *Offerings*.

That's the story action, the bare bones. But with Alice Munro the difference between the bare bones of the story and the way she organizes the bones and flesh of her text is enormous. Munro's telling extends to roughly 9,000 words which she splits up into six numbered sections. Each section begins with an epigraph, a four or five-line stanza from one of Meda's poems. The chronology of the text extends from 1840, the year Meda was born, to the mid-1980s when the story was written (a first-person narrator, someone like Alice Munro herself, tells the story from the notional present). But the crucial events of the story, as I say, take place over a weekend in August, 1879.

The first section of text deals, essay-like, with Meda's slim volume of poems; section II describes her little southern Ontario town in 1879; section III introduces the widower Jarvis Poulter and his half-hearted interest in Meda; in the fourth section, Meda wakes to the sound of wailing and fighting in the backyard, summons Jarvis and unmans him, so to speak, with a show of fluttery weakness; in the fifth section, she gets stoned and leaves the note pinned to her front door, rejecting Poulter's sudden romantic overture; and section VI is aftermath: Meda's 1903 obituary and the authorial narrator's ruminations on rescuing the experience of the past. The main action is concentrated in two of the six sections; the first two sections read like essays; and the last section contains two obituaries and some paragraphs of narrator reflection rooted in the present, the time of writing.

By "main action" I mean plot, a structure of desire and resistance (conflict) in which the same desire and the same resistance meet in a series of actions (events). Because her story organization is heterodox, Alice Munro is almost always precise and transparent in terms of her desire-resistance patterns. The first plot event in "Meneseteung" is a composite of Jarvis's half-hearted courtship described in the third section. Meda's concrete desire is enunciated in the following sentences:

> [My italics] And she is thinking of him. She doesn't want to get her hopes up too much, she doesn't want to make a fool of herself. *She would like a signal.*

The notion of what this signal might be is refined a few lines later.

Nor does he call for her, and walk with her *to* church on Sunday mornings. *That would be a declaration.*

In section IV, at the climax of the Sunday morning scene with the drunk woman behind Meda's house, in a burst of (comic) Canadian machismo, Jarvis gives her the signal she has been waiting for.

> He is sufficiently stirred by her loosened hair—prematurely gray but thick and soft—her flushed face, her light clothing, which nobody but a husband should see. And by her indiscretion, her agitation, her foolishness, her need?
>
> "I will call on you later," he says to her. *"I will walk with you to church."*

However at this stage even Meda's body is telling her that this is no longer the signal she wants; in section V, she rushes away from Jarvis to the privy, then leaves a note on the door politely rejecting his offer. The accent on the word "signal" has shifted; Meda still wants a signal but of a different kind. When it comes, the sign is inside her own heart. Thus the plot sequence is completed when, in a drugged dream-state, she looks into the "river of her mind" and imagines the crocheted roses in her table cloth floating.

> They look bunchy and foolish, her mother's crocheted roses—they don't look much like real flowers. But their effort, their floating independence, their pleasure in their silly selves, does seem to her so admirable.
>
> *A hopeful sign.*

How does Munro make this heterodox structure work? So much preamble and aftermath, the plot condensed into a narrow band of text? The answer lies in the way she deploys, develops, elaborates, and ramifies basic structural devices and the way she uses this elaboration to create rhythms, rhymes, reminders, echoes, antagonisms, under-meanings, and semantic loops— action and drama at the level of text and syntax. She uses resonating structures so that various parts of the text echo off each other. She uses a complex point of view structure to create variety and contrast in the types of text threaded through the narrative (and thus a variety of perspectives). She dances with time. She creates action, conflict, and emotion even in those parts of the story that are not directly related to plot. In other words, the set-up, backfill, and aftermath are more than set-up, backfill, and aftermath; the essays are not just essays; they are written into the text as what I call ancillary devices, devices for elaborating, extending, complicating, and repeating aspects of the main plot structure of the story. While they do add information and explanation, I suspect their real function is to create complex rhythmic and aesthetic effects which make the story grander and yet far more ironic than any mere summary can intimate.

Take that elusive point of view, for instance. Unstudied readers tend to think of point of view as consistent and monolithic. They barely give it a second thought. Munro explodes the notion of consistent point of view. The whole story is told by a first person narrator who comes into the text three times. The first mention occurs glancingly in the second paragraph ("... that makes me see ..."), the second occurs more emphatically in a one-sentence paragraph in section II ("I read about that life in the *Vidette*.") and the third, most insistently, through the final paragraphs of section VI, each beginning with "I." The notional set-up here is that the authorial narrator, someone like Alice Munro, has researched Meda's life, read the local newspaper, read Meda's poems, visited the family graves, and is writing the story.

However most of the story is written in a fluid third person, that first person authorial narrator transforming into the objective observer describing Meda's book of poems and the wry interpreter of the village newspaper the *Vidette* ("This kind of thing pops up in the *Vidette* all the time. May they surmise, and is this courting?") while here and there modulating into a third person plural corporate point of view (the townspeople) and finally into a close third person single character point of view focused very tightly on Meda (and once or twice, even in Jarvis Poulter's mind). But even the third person plural structure has gradations of attack. It shifts from strict synopses of the *Vidette* to third person plural ("People talk about . . ." "All he has told them . . .") and finally to a group interior monologue, a variation of free indirect discourse ("Anyway, it's five years since her book was published, so perhaps she has got over that. Perhaps it was the proud, bookish father encouraging her?"). It's lovely to watch Munro's structural segues. Here's an example of a shift from third plural to third singular in three sentences:

> Everyone takes it for granted that Almeda Roth is thinking of Jarvis Poulter as a husband and would say yes if he asked her. And she is thinking of him. She doesn't want to get her hopes up too much . . .

This is not to mention the point of view shifts involved in the inter-textual play of narrative and quotation that is one of Munro's hallmark devices. In "Meneseteung" she provides Meda's first person narrative in the form of a quotation from the preface to her book, also quotations from the village paper, the *Vidette*, including the obituaries of both main characters, and stanzas from Meda's poems along with a sprinkling of poem titles (the title of the story is a reference to the title of one of the poems). Quotation is a device for varying point of view within a text, not to be overlooked just because, on one level, it is so obvious.

Nor does it take into account another favourite Munro device, something I call the device of imaginative reconstruction: this refers to a moment in the text when the point of view shifts into a purely hypothetical or imagined mode and relates events that may or may not have happened at all.

> Instead of calling for her and walking her to church, Jarvis Poulter might make another, more venturesome declaration. He could hire a horse and take her for a drive out to the country. If he did this, she would be both glad and sorry. . . .

These sentences introduce a long paragraph of narrative summary of an event between Meda and Jarvis that never takes place. The modal verbs "might" and "could" provide the syntactic frame.

Another example occurs when the authorial narrator describes Jarvis Poulter for the first time. Lacking photographs, she imagines what he looks like in a series of rhetorical questions (the syntactic frame device), the question marks indicating the purely speculative quality of the details which nevertheless enter the reader's mind as story-fact.

> This is a decent citizen, prosperous: a tall—slightly paunchy?—man in a dark suit with polished boots. A beard? Black hair streaked with gray. A severe and self-possessed air, and a large pale wart among the bushy hairs of one eyebrow?

The author uses the device of imaginative reconstruction to insert pictures (fictions within fiction) in the reader's mind, modulating in and out of strong narrative authority using grammar (framing hypothetical text syntactically; syntactic framing is a device you often see in Munro stories).

The effect of these point of view shifts, the constant fluidity of structure, is to create a relativity machine within the text, the beat of authority skipping from sentence to sentence, more or less subverting what has gone before. This is action at the level of point of view, conflict at the level of discourse; no one is giving the conclusive picture; the work of art is not a reality but a domain of shifting and competing relations. Vladimir Nabokov says somewhere that we read with our spines; like him, I am a straight materialist when it comes to the effect of reading on the reader. Being forced to play the scales, to shift from point of view to point of view, causes fizz in the networks, causes the brain, suddenly, to be more alive in ways that are at once disconcerting, pleasurable, and illuminating.

The same goes for the way Munro manipulates and elaborates her time structure. In every story, there is an objective time scale that is chronological and runs from the very first event indicated within the text to the very last, and, in contrast, there is the way the author actually deploys time in the narrative (what I think of as the time flow). In "Meneseteung" Munro controls time with surgical precision. The objective chronology runs from 1840, when Meda is born, to the mid-1980s when the story was written. Munro carefully dates the major events in between. 1865, Meda's photograph taken. 1873, Meda's book published. August, 1879, the incident with Jarvis and the drunk woman. 1903, Meda dies. By calculations based on internal evidence (e.g. "My sister was eleven and my brother nine.") we obtain more dates. 1854, Meda's family moves from Kingston to the frontier village. 1857, her two younger siblings die of a prevalent fever. 1860, her mother dies. 1872, her father dies. These dates, in themselves, begin to tell a story.

But time in a story never flows in a straight line; it loops and eddies and suddenly compresses in a spasm of action, then stretches out again. "Meneseteung," for example, begins in the authorial present with a description of Meda's book of poems as if held in the narrator's hands ("Gold lettering on a dull-blue cover."), then swoops back to the 1870s with a quote from the *Vidette* and then, more precisely, dates when the book was written and when the author's photograph was taken. In this first paragraph, Munro is teaching us to read the time shifts that characterize much of the text that follows.

In the second paragraph, through the photo, we see Meda in 1865. In the third paragraph, Munro's narrator quotes from Meda's preface (written prior to 1873) which loops dizzyingly through the whole of Meda's life from 1840 to 1873. The last few paragraphs of this first section summarize individual poems that limn events in Meda's life and, though undated, clearly loop back over the life again (Meda playing games with her brother and sister, the children making snow angels, Meda visiting the family graves). Each time these poems or events are referenced in the text (including those stanzas used as epigraphs), they send the reader's mind (remind the reader) back to an earlier time. This reminding creates a sort of temporal jazz; the reader's mind is constantly dashing from one moment to some other moment and simultaneously referring to that objective chronology.

In terms of time flow, Munro often uses a lovely little device I call the then/now construction, a grammatical structure that juxtaposes two moments in such a way as to imply change (story) over time. Sometimes authors use the words "then" and "now," and sometimes the words are only implied. Here is a masterful example of a then/now with intervening moments deftly added (as technique, it's breathtaking).

> [my italics and bracket notes] *In 1879* [then], Almeda Roth *was* still living in the house at the corner of Pearl and Dufferin streets, the house her father *had built* for his family [ca. 1854]. The house *is there today* [now, ca. 1985]: the manager of the liquor store lives in it. It's covered with aluminum siding; a closed-in porch has replaced the

veranda [then, 1879]. The woodshed, the fence, the gates, the privy, the barn—all these are gone [now, 1985]. A photograph *taken in the eighteen-eighties* [then, 1880s] shows them all in place. The house and fence look a little shabby, in need of paint . . . No big shade tree is in sight, and, in fact, the tall elms that overshadowed the town *until the nineteen-fifties* [1950s], as well as the maples that shade it *now* [now obviously, 1985] are skinny young trees [then, 1880s]. . . .

Note especially the final arabesque flurry which swoops the reader from 1885 to 1955 to 1985 and back to 1885 in less than one sentence. As with those bravura point of view shifts, I am not sure the general reader notices this kind of authorial stick-handling, though, again, I suspect it has the same neural effect on the brain as doing loop-de-loops in a biplane without a seatbelt (today, I like the word "fizz"). But Munro's precise and adamantine control assures the reader that the story's temporal matrix is as consistent and reliable as a ticking clock.

The time structures I've mentioned so far have little to do with the hoary ideas of scene and summary in which time is conceived of as being either slowed and drawn out (scene) or speeded up as in fast-forwarding (summary). If you think of summary as nothing but a plodding rehearsal of time past, you miss the point of the phantasmagoric loops and eddies in a narrative like "Meneseteung." Munro does speed up time, covering over a hundred and forty years in a few pages. But the techniques she deploys do more than just fill in the blanks; she forces the reader to experience the passage of time, to become conscious of change, of mutability, and to taste the ironic aspect of death that dogs all history.

Munro does, of course, slow the moment; in fact, the first four sections of the story create the effect of a step-by-step deceleration (somewhat paralleling the progressive tightening of the point of view) until we reach the fourth section which begins with Meda shocked awake on a hot August Saturday night by the drunken rumpus in the back street behind her house. She sleeps, then wakes on Sunday morning and discovers the body and runs for help. The dialogue scene that follows, between Jarvis, Meda and the resuscitated drunk, is the longest in the story, a climax of imagined horror—sordid, shocking, surprising (and somehow more real because it's sordid, shocking, and surprising), and hilarious. The drunken woman is awful, an image of filth, poverty, and drunken animal sexuality (somehow this phrase gives animals a bad name). Jarvis is upright, bourgeois, masculine, and despicable. Meda is in shock; she has to use the outhouse. Then suddenly Jarvis is aroused. He finally sees Meda as a possible sex object and marriage option. He announces that he will walk her to church. (The fact that Alice Munro comprehends and can convey the complex and deeply comic conditions of male arousal in Jarvis's case alone justifies calling her a genius in my books.)

This scene is the notional climax of the story, but Munro is a master of syncopation, and, besides, the story isn't about Jarvis Poulter's arousal. In this scene, Meda gets what the text has told us she wants ("She would like a signal."), but by this stage she realizes she doesn't want it (a man and a man's reality), and so in the fifth section of the story she must escape from the ogre of her author's creation. In the fifth section, time speeds up slightly; a whole day passes in a series of small dreamy scenes and snippets, mostly Meda's actions and thoughts as she gets more and more stoned on nerve medicine, skillfully punctuated by a stream of minute domestic acts, external impressions, and time markers.

> As soon as Jarvis Poulter has gone . . . She closes . . . she writes [and leaves a note for Jarvis on the door] . . . She sticks . . . She locks . . . she builds a fire . . . She boils water

. . . several dark drops of nerve medicine . . . She is still sitting there when the horses start to go by on the way to church, stirring up clouds of dust. The roads will be getting hot as ashes [Jarvis comes and goes from the veranda] . . . Then the clock in the hall strikes twelve and an hour has passed. . . . The house is getting hot. She drinks more tea and adds more medicine . . . She doesn't leave the room until dusk, when she goes out to the privy again . . .

The climax of this fifth section, the true climax of the story, is what takes place in Meda's mind as she sits in her dining room sipping laudanum and tea after Jarvis has retreated from the veranda. The relevant text begins with Meda looking out ("Her surroundings—some of her surroundings—in the dining room are these . . ."), but then she peers inward and she is stoned and what floods the page is an intense and surreal confluence (the story is named for a river, after all, and the thoughts are motivated by emotional shock, hormones, opium, and poetry) of physical detail, image, memory, and theme that is at once the secret, hidden life of Almeda Roth and a bravura meditation on life, poetry, the self, language, and metaphysics.

It's fascinating to realize that this climactic confluence is not so much an action on a plot line as an eruption of Meda's inner experience provoked by the plot. And what it amounts to in terms of story construction is an intersection of various images, motifs, and patterns already precisely adumbrated in the text. Munro seems to realize that the inner life of a man or a woman is also a text, that in our secret hearts we are talking to ourselves, muttering, declaiming; at its deepest point this is our experience of experience. In this case, she constructs her story so that the inner text of Meda's heart cunningly reflects and pulls together the outer text of the story. Here we rediscover the old truth that repetition is the heart of art.

Take Meda's poems. They are not part of the surface drama of the story. They were written long before she meets Jarvis Poulter. They are contained in a book which we glimpse ("Gold lettering on a dull-blue cover.") in the first line of the story ("*Offerings*, the book is called.") The first section of the story further contains three paragraphs of quotation from Meda's preface to the book and then a list of poems: "Children at Their Games," "The Gypsy Fair," "A Visit to My Family," "Angels in the Snow," "Champlain at the Mouth of the Meneseteung." The poem titles pick up family background motifs just mentioned in the prefatory material (brother and sister, their deaths). The river name, Meneseteung, repeats the title of the story. In the next seven paragraphs, Munro glosses each of the listed poems, nailing the content to an experience from Meda's life (again, brother and sister, their deaths). The title of the Meneseteung poem is repeated and glossed: "This poem celebrates the popular, untrue belief that the explorer sailed down the eastern shore of Lake Huron and landed at the mouth of the major river." And, of course, we remember that each of these poems is again referenced in the epigraphs that begin the story sections (it's not difficult to puzzle out which stanza comes from which poem). At this stage, the astute reader realizes that he is witnessing the construction of a major image pattern, part of the organization of the story as a whole, a vehicle for meaning and aesthetic effect (rhythm, cohesion), that is also somehow separate from the dramatic action of the story.

Image (or word) patterns begin with mere repetition, accumulate meaning by association and juxtaposition, splinter or ramify, sending out subsidiary branch patterns, and, finally, discover occasions for recombination or intersection of the various branches in what I call tie-in lines. Often, as in this case, the primary image pattern is tipped in the story title, a further sign that the image pattern controls development and meaning within the text (in a sense, the title tells us the story is more about the image than the plot). In "Meneseteung," we have something faintly reminiscent of the rhetorical device of *ekphrasis*, though here the work of art being decoded as an element of the meaning of the whole is not a painting or a statue but a book of poems. The words "Meneseteung," "river," "book," "poem," and "poet" appear as a branched constellation at the center of the story "Meneseteung."

Once you begin to tease apart the branching patterns and spot the relevant associations, some fascinating story elements begin to appear. Given the title (and the way things work out in the fifth section), "Meneseteung" is the root pattern; "Meneseteung" is a river, a poem in a book, a reference to a popular but mistaken historical belief, the title of a story. "Book" is mentioned in the first line of the story and leads along a wonderful line of "bookishness," paternal influence and popular prejudice:

> [my italics] . . . preface to her *book*, "my *father* . . . My *father* was a harness-maker by trade, but a *cultivated* man who could quote by heart from the *Bible*, *Shakespeare*, and *the writings of Edmund Burke* . . ."

> But why was she *passed over* in her earlier, more marriageable years . . . All that *reading and poetry*—it seemed more of a *drawback*, a *barrier*, an *obsession*, in the young girl than in the middle-aged woman, who needed something, after all, to *fill her time*. Anyway, it's five years since her *book* was published, so perhaps she has *got over* that. Perhaps it was the *proud, bookish father*, encouraging her?

Note how the image accumulates a precise list of associations (linked words) and also, how, depending on point of view, the list varies: what Meda sees as "cultivated" the town sees as "proud" and "bookish." Word lists like this are a very common structure in Alice Munro stories, and, as in this instance, she often develops contrasting words lists (Meda's list of associations with books and poetry v. the town's list; Meda's list of geographical associations v. Jarvis's list; words associated with the proper part of town along Dufferin Street v. words associated with the poor part of town along Pearl Street—of course, Meda's house sits at the corner of Dufferin and Pearl). And the effect of these branching image patterns and their associated (conflict-driven) word lists is an extremely complicated and dense criss-cross matrix of interconnected references that echo in the reader's mind and construct a disciplined and precise semblance of experience.

This matrix of cross-reference is all the more alive, as it were, because it is inscribed with conflict; the competing points of view strive for interpretive primacy—at the end of the story which list of associations will own the image? This conflict plays out in the reader's mind, but, more significantly, it plays out in Meda's mind and is embodied, through story action, in her near acceptance of Jarvis Poulter as a suitor. This is Alice Munro's version of Mikhail Bakhtin's vision of the novel as a battle of discourses, which is also a battle to subvert some old or conventional or authoritative discourse. In "Meneseteung," Meda Roth battles for the meaning of the book, of poetry, of her father, of the land, and of her self against the popular, conventional discourse of the townspeople and the *Vidette* and against the bourgeois male, commercial discourse of Jarvis Poulter.

> [my italics] He could hire a horse and take her for a drive out to the country. If he did this, she would be *both glad and sorry. Glad* to be beside him, driven by him, receiving this attention from him in front of the world. *And sorry* to have the *countryside removed from her, filmed over, in a way, by his talk and his preoccupations. The countryside that she has written about in her poems actually takes diligence and determination to see.*

In this passage, Meda and Jarvis compete over who will get to describe the "countryside." Consciousness is a text; the words you use colour your experience. It takes diligence, determination, and poetry to recover experience from the conventional. And the word "countryside" here is not an isolate; Munro has carefully threaded landscape and countryside through the story as a branch of the poem-book-Meneseteung pattern. It begins in the first section with that poem "The Passing of the Old Forest" glossed as "a list of all the trees—their names, appearance, and uses—that were cut down in the original forest . . ." which later becomes (reflecting Jarvis's values) "[a] raw countryside just wrenched from the forest . . ."

> [my italics] The meandering *creeks* have been straightened, turned into *ditches* . . . The *trees* have all been cleared back to *woodlots*. And the woodlots are all second growth . . . the grand barns that are to *dominate* the *countryside* for the next hundred years are just beginning to be built—

In truth, everywhere you look in an Alice Munro story there is conflict and change. No word sits by itself; instead, each word vibrates in a dozen relationships with other words, repeating, competing, dominating, wrenching, transforming, shading, and subverting.

The moment of climax for all this comes, as I say, not with Jarvis's priapic epiphany (I use the word ironically) and sudden access of ardour, nor when the poetess rejects him, but when Meda locks herself in her house and gets stoned. At this point she shuts out the discourse of the conventional Others (Jarvis, the town) and attends first to her surroundings which seem "charged with life, ready to move and flow and alter." Note the word "flow" because presently the "glowing and swelling" of things begin to "suggest words," and the words begin to suggest "Poems, even. Yes, again, poems. Or one poem." And that one poem will contain all the poems Meda has written and all the events of the story.

Here Munro inserts a classic rehearsal device, a piece of text in which previous events are recapitulated, the story rehearsed (a repetitive structure that has the effect of reminding the reader of the salient points and also giving a kind of rhythmic kick that announces the approaching end of the narrative):

> [my italics and bracket notes] . . . one very great *poem* that will contain everything . . . *Stars and flowers and birds and trees and angels in the snow and dead children at twilight*— that is not the half of it. You have to get in *the obscene racket on Pearl Street and the polished toe of Jarvis Poulter's boot and the plucked chicken haunch and its blue-black flower*. Almeda is a long way now from human sympathies . . . [here Munro inserts some lines on Meda's problematic conventional alternatives for dramatic effect, also a reference to grape jelly, another image pattern that has some sly connection with menstruation—there is no end to this] . . . She has to think of so many things at once—*Champlain and the naked Indians and the salt deep in the earth*. . . .

Munro follows the rehearsal of events with a new twist on the things-to-words-to-poems-to-everything-in-one-poem pattern. It's an amazing passage, the climax of the story's linguistic acceleration, the electrical charge, transferred along the image lines (networks) from the very beginning of the story, from the title, in fact, to this point. Technically, it's a simple modulation of the image pattern that starts with the word "channel" used as a double figure; first, as a conventional metaphor (as in "channeling my energy"), and, second, as a pun. "Channel" has the magical effect of turning the poem into a river, the Menesete-ung, a mighty poem-river, an image of all things, as it were, even the story itself (it is the title, after all). And then the "river" turns figurative and becomes "the river of her mind."

> [my italics] All this can be borne only if it is *channeled* into a *poem*, and the word "*channeled*" is appropriate, because the *name* of the *poem* will be "The *Meneseteung*." The *name* of the *poem* is the *name* of the *river*. No, in fact, it is the *river*, the *Meneseteung*, that is the *poem*—with its deep holes and rapids and blissful pools under the summer trees . . . Almeda looks deep, deep into *the river of her mind*. . . .

This is the confluence of image patterns, the point at which the battle of discourses ceases and Meda performs the mythic rite of the naming of experience; she reclaims forever her self, her poems, and her countryside.

What Alice Munro reads, I have now idea. But the philosophy, the theory, behind her plots and patterns is clear, complex, and very contemporary. As you might expect from a writer so at home in language, the mind is a text, experience a flow of words. The struggle within every story, the struggle for identity, is always a battle for the word, the authority to give names. Perhaps all writers think this way in their hearts. And whatever is real beyond the words is problematic. In fact, it doesn't matter. All the devices I have discussed so far in relation to this story—fluid point of view, time flow, and image patterning as deployed by Munro—serve only to relativize the object, make the object a moment of contest, never at rest. Every word in "Meneseteung" is restless and alive. And even at the point of confluence, when Meda lets herself sink into the river of her mind—Menesete-ung—Alice Munro is there with her spade, ready to turn the earth of the story one more time.

In the last section of the story, Munro jumps ahead twenty-four years to 1903; the battle of discourses cranks up again; she quotes Meda's obituary in the *Vidette*:

> [my italics] . . . the *mind* of this fine person had become somewhat *clouded* and her behaviour, in consequence, somewhat *rash and unusual.* Her attention to *decorum* and to the *care and adornment* of her person had suffered, to the degree that she had become, in the eyes of those mindful of her former *pride and daintiness,* a familiar *eccentric,* or even, sadly, *a figure of fun.*

Meda is dead and the townspeople get the final word as to her "mind." There are two things to notice here. First, Munro is extending the competing patterns already figured into the text beyond the climax; this is an example of her style of syncopation—she always adds a beat at the end of the phrase, always undercuts the conclusion. In 1879, subjectively, Meda may have won the war, but from a different point of view (in Munro stories, there is always another point of view), she merely becomes an eccentric figure of fun. In terms of the story, the state of her "mind" remains in play.

Second, this is also an example of a different sort of repetition, what I call book-ending (as in book-ends or brackets), which is also a sort of structural *epanalepsis.* The words of the obituary echo, with emphasis, sentiments expressed in the opening paragraph of the story:

> The local paper, the *Vidette*, referred to her as "our poetess." There seems to be a mixture of respect and contempt, both for her calling and for her sex—or for their predictable conjuncture.

The smug condescension dripping from those quotation marks encode the story from beginning to end with an attitude of amused dismissiveness. Being a "poetess" and unmarried, Meda never achieves a position of significance within her community; her experience never recognized as a legitimate experience.

At this point the battle for Meda's mind and the soul of the story seems lost. Note that we have gone far beyond the plot interest here; Meda has escaped Jarvis's attentions; both characters are dead; but the conflict of patterns and discourses continues. This is a fascinating moment: our concern is no longer with the characters; at this point we are more interested in the battle of discourses than we are in how the plot action turned out. We want to know what conclusion the story comes to— about Meda, Meda's mind and, ultimately, about itself.

Munro nails Meda's descent on the social scale of significance with another repetition—so pretty a thing I can't bear not mentioning it. In the second section of the story, that description of Meda's town, Munro tells the story of Queen Aggie, "an old woman, a drunk" whom the village boys would harass, riding her around in a wheelbarrow (oh, the wheelbarrow pattern!) and dumping her into a ditch to sober up. Queen Aggie prefigures the drunken woman in Meda's backyard in the fourth section, but she also prefigures Meda's death as described in the *Vidette*—chased by village louts, the old biddy tumbles into a swamp (the swamp pattern!), catches cold and dies.

The last paragraphs of the story fall to the authorial narrator, Alice Munro's first-person stand-in, in a sense, the umpire. She looks at the microfilm, hefts the book, visits the cemetery and, with some difficulty, finds Meda's gravestone.

> . . . I began pulling grass and scrabbling in the dirt with my bare hands. Soon I felt the stone and knew that I was right.

The reader should be reminded here that it "takes diligence and determination to see." As she angles towards her ending, Munro, as her alter ago, muses on what she thinks she knows about Meda Roth, whether anyone else could figure it out, whether it's even true. But then she thinks:

> [my italics] People are *curious. A few people* are. They will be driven to find things out, even trivial things. They will *put things together*, knowing all along *they may be mistaken*. You see them going around with notebooks, scraping the dirt off the gravestones, reading microfilm, just in the hope of seeing *this trickle in time*, making *a connection, rescuing one thing from the rubbish*.

The phrase "this trickle in time" is gorgeous, the sort of authorial nudge that sets up the hair on the back of your neck. It extends the river-poem-Meneseteung-mind pattern one last step. Nearly the final words of the story, the phrase washes back over the text as a whole, the little repetitive points of contact flashing like streetlights. The passage invites readers to make connections, put things together, and rescue Meda's experience from the rubbish of conventional judgement. There is this allegorical element in everything Alice Munro writes; she is always teaching readers how to read her stories as she writes them; there are always connections to be made.

The trickle in time is the Meneseteung, the great poem-river of Meda's mind, rescued from forgetfulness and conventional opinion by the curious narrator (much as Meda has to rescue her own experience from conventional expectation and judgement). The allegory is gentle; the mind is the hero and poet laureate of its own experience. Experience is not a passive act; it takes diligence and determination to identify, name and own the facts of one's existence. The enemy is conventional language; the antidote is poetry and mild intoxicants. The result may not be authentic in an objective sense. Munro, true to the flux and flow of her own narrative, is careful to suggest experience thus earned may be faulty. ("I may have got it wrong.") In a final act of subversion, she seems to say that reality itself is a fiction, that what we rescue with poetry is, well, poetry. As Meda, stoned, watches trippy, animated roses and tombstones, the narrator opines:

> She doesn't mistake that for reality, and neither does she mistake anything else for reality, and that is how she knows that she is sane.

HOW TO READ A
MARK ANTHONY JARMAN
STORY

THOUGH OFTEN RISING out of situations that are violent or bizarre or both, Mark Jarman's story lines tend to be minimal, just enough plausible action to jump-start the engine of his verbal inventiveness. And this verbal inventiveness is somehow tied to voice—most of Jarman's stories are written in the first person, as monologues in the point of view of characters under stress, their synapses sparking at high voltage with the effort to stay hip or cool or maintain "dignity" as the manic burn victim calls it in "Burn Man on a Texas Porch."

"Burn Man on a Texas Porch" is the story of a British Columbia bureaucrat horribly disfigured in a propane tank explosion while on vacation. After recovering in the Royal Jubilee burn unit, Burn Man grows a beard to cover his face and finds employment appearing in disguises (clown, ape, moose). Since he can't have a normal relationship any longer, he hires Cindi, an escort, to have sex with him. He drinks in bars and one night watches a fight in which an off-duty policeman is kicked to death. Through all this he sorts through memories: 1) memories of childhood: reading about Canadian sailors burning in the North Atlantic, being sunburned in Penticton, an aunt peeling off a patch of sunburned skin; 2) memories of a story a golf buddy told him about finding a dead scuba diver in the woods after a forest fire; 3) and memories of a brief love affair with a Texas woman who sings Emmy-Lou Harris songs in a band.

The quintessential Jarman moment takes place early in this story. The protagonist is lurching around a tourist campsite in flames after a propane tank blows up inside his rented trailer. He thinks to himself: "I'm okay, okay, will be fine except I'm hoovering all the oxygen around me, and I'm burning like a circus poster, flames taking more and more of my shape—am I moving or are they? I am hooked into fire, I am hysterical light issuing beast noises in a world of smoke." This is a horrific encounter, but the narrator's prime reaction seems to be a sheepish embarrassment occasioned by the scene he is making, and he hastens to reassure his audience (sleepy campers, teens in pajamas, and the reader) even as, in some other psychic quandrant, he is consumed by flames. This is the voice of beleaguered cool, the rhetorical position out of which many of Jarman's stories operate.

Now look more closely at what happens in this passage. It's all one sentence, a twisty sentence, careening along the cusp of correct syntax but in many ways a paradigm of Jarman's style. First, try to imagine how else he might have written this passage, how realistically he might have tried to present the feelings of a man being burned alive, how banal and expected that might be. Then note how he begins: the natural-sounding dialogue, banal in itself, though speeded up, truncated, by the use of repetition and ellipsis. The passage turns on the next word "except" which creates what I call, when I teach, a but-construction, that is the use of the word "but" or cognate to create contrast or conflict between what comes before and what comes after. The passage works as an ironic juxtaposition of the burning man trying to maintain his cool before a crowd of gawking onlookers and the man whose self is dissolving into flames from which issue those incoherent beast noises.

After "except," the sentence begins to accrete horror and power. Jarman has a talent for finding the precise, if odd, word. Here "hoovering," which comes from Hoover, a manufacturer of vacuum cleaners, and a common enough, if slightly old-fashioned, use of the word as a verb, lets the reader know the sentence is beginning to twist. Already, in order to read the sentence, the reader has to unpack hoovering, remember vacuum cleaners, vacuuming, sucking, and the fact that fire sucks oxygen out of the air. And it's "I" who is doing the hoovering, not the flames.

Then a comma-plus-conjunction-"and" followed by a parallel construction "I'm burning like a circus poster" which provides a gloss on hoovering and extends the meaning with the peculiar simile (think: lions and tigers leap through rings of fire). Then a variation of the parallel: "flames taking over more and more of my shape"; followed by a long dash signaling a parenthetical intrusion or interruption, and a rhetorical question which ties "I" and the flames together and inverts the "I am" to "am I." So we get a kind of rhythmic forward motion propelled by the parallel constructions, suddenly, grammatically, derailed and interrupted (conflict, drama, at the level of syntax) by the long dash and the question.

And rather than stop there, rather than slow the sentence, Jarman continues with the assertion "I am hooked into fire"— again with the odd verb "hooked"—followed by a parallel assertion: "I am hysterical light issuing beast noises in a world of smoke." Thus the sentence as a whole begins with a colloquial reassurance which is denied in the next breath ("except"), this denial moving forward by progressive parallels to the syntactic eruption of the long dash plus rhetorical question. This eruption knots or pauses the sentence, which hangs a moment on the question mark, then resolves itself in the twin assertions.

The last clause is a marvel of striking word choice and surprising construction. First the psychological adjective "hysterical" applied to the noun "light"; then the noun "beast" twisted syntactically into an adjective modifying the noun "noises." And, in between, the strange present participle "issuing," a verb which in its transitive form means "to publish, send forth, put into circulation," a use of the word which, in this context, is bizarre, poetic and highly unsettling. The final phrase "in a world of smoke" is both apt and yet adds to the surreality of the clause; in this clause, the narrator has lost his identity, his identity has become the flames. Note also the rhythmic quality that evolves out of the repetitions of words and of grammatical constructions. The last clause caps the rising rhythm of the sentence as a whole with a stately march of anapests and iambs. "I am hysterical light issuing beast noises in a world of smoke."

Okay, one sentence. Here is a brief list of some of the other devices one can find Jarman using to add interest to his narratives:

The striking simile: ". . . blew the camper door off and split the tin walls where they met *like shy strangers kissing* . . .";

puns: "The skin is the largest *organ*; mine's a little out of tune";

apostrophe: "O, I am ill at these numbers";

chiasmus (modified): "Propane slept in the tank and propane leaked while I slept . . ."

external literary/cultural references: Shakespeare's *Othello*, Stevie Smith, pop music, *War and Peace*, *Moby Dick*,

I Love Lucy, Tristan and Isolde, One Flew Over the Cuckoo's Nest, Bonanza. In each case, the reference introduces another text, a separate discourse, which the reader mentally juxtaposes with the narrative of the story;

parenthetical intrusions (using brackets, commas or long dashes): ". . . flames gathering and glittering on my shoulders (Cool, the teens think secretly) . . ." Here the brackets enclose a discourse that seems to break point of view, jump outside the head of the narrating I and enter the heads of the teenagers watching him burn. ". . . Cindi shows me a photo of herself as a little girl in a little bathing suit at the beach (*Yes that's me in the photo!*)." ". . . blabbing over Gram Parsons and Emmylou (*One like you should be—miles and miles away from me*), . . ." "On Saturdays I wave white gloves to passing cars—dark shark-like taxis, myopic headlights—and helium balloons with smiley faces bump my wrecked and now abandoned mouth. (*Where have all the old finned cars swum to?*)";

word repetition with changed meaning (isolexism): "Doors blow off the *rented* camper, spinning under the sulphur sun, and I too am sent out into red *rented* sunlight . . ." ". . . my *fat* burning like red wax, *fat* in the fire now . . ." ". . . I cracked jokes like delicate quails eggs: You can't fire me, I already *quit*. Then I *quit* cracking jokes." "New *careers* in fire and oxygen, *careering* and hammering through the Dolomite campground . . ." "I was *fast*. I stood *fast*.";

word repetition where the spelling, sound and meaning change sequentially: ". . . their *legions* and *lesions* and *lessons* . . ." "I *napped* and the propane fire *snapped* my skin, *remapped* me." ". . . washed away original *sin*, she held my perfect skin, my original *skin*."

He uses word repetition in classic rhetorical structures: for example, Jarman will end one passage or paragraph with a word or a phrase and begin the next passage or paragraph with the same word (*anadiplosis*).

> . . . I didn't call that number. I don't live in the metro area. I'm not one of the *chosen*.
>   Once, maybe, I was *chosen*, necking on the Hopper porch . . .

Or he will begin a passage or a paragraph with a word or phrase and end the passage with the same word or phrase (a variation of *epanalepsis*).

> *Dignity is essential.* I attempt to impart to a passing priest, but I start coughing like a moron. Drugs too, I finally sputter. *Essential!* He moves on. Brother, sister, I may appear in ape costume at your apartment door, will deliver a singing telegram in a serviceable tenor. My grey rabbit suit needs a little bleach. *Dignity is essential.*

> *I who loved the status quo,* liked things to stay the same even when they were bad . . . Then the camper door flies off: Kablooie! Goodbye Louie. *I who loved the status quo.*

> She coughed. Uh, I'm *cool with that*, she claimed.
>   So Cindi and I set up our first date.
>   My escort dresses as the nurse in white, her hands, her crisp uniform glowing in the rec room. All of us risk something, dress as something: ape, clown, worker, Cindi, citizen, *cool with that.*

Flame created me with its sobering sound. Wake up, flame whispered in my ear, like a woman on a porch . . . (skip over a paragraph and a half) . . .

The woman on the Texas porch said my skin was soft and that she loved the smell. No one ever said that before, and no one said it after. *She created me.*

In the last passage, the variation "flame"-to-"she" and the simile "like a woman on a porch" nail a strange and unsettling connection Jarman wants to make between the fire which changed Burn Man forever and his romantic brush with the woman on the Texas porch which preceded it. This romantic brush idea ties in with a "desire" pattern: ". . . for Burn Man is not burnt everywhere, still has some desires . . ." "Here's an ad in *Now* magazine I didn't recall: 'FIRE & DESIRE, Sensuous Centrefold Girls, HOT fall Specials . . ." "I still have that shy desire for the right fire . . ." Here, as in many portions of a Jarman text, there is very little plot action, but amazing amounts of verbal action—connections, parallels, contrasts, variations. This passage adds no action to the story, does not advance character, and is ambiguous as to meaning. But it creates resonance and texture and a feeling that there is more here than the surface story.

Another sort of repetition Jarman uses is an extended word pattern. In this case, fire is the primary pattern. Jarman begins the story with Burn Man catching "fire." Words like "flames" "smoke" and "burn" occur repeatedly as a natural part of the scene description as it develops. But they also strike off as subsidiary patterns from the root fire-pattern.

Track "burn," for example. Starts on the second page of the story: "I'm *burning* like a circus poster . . ." ". . . but soon the tent is melting (sets up a "melt" pattern), merrily *burning* with me . . ." "Tourists *burn* their hands . . ." Then the narrator becomes Burn Man. "At some point in this year of our Lord I began to refer to myself in third person, as a double: *Burn Man* enters the Royal Jubilee *burn* unit, *Burn Man* enters the saline painful sea. *Burn Man* reads . . ." (The Burn Man pattern splinters off—"splinter" is the word Viktor Shklovsky uses to describe the splitting off of sub-patterns from the root—a Rocket Man sub-pattern: "I spill Swedish and Russian vodka into my morning coffee now (*rocket* fuel for *Rocket Man*)" which is re-touched in the last sentence of the story when ". . . a famous scuba diver *rockets* like a lost dark god . . ." ". . . carried me in the *burnt* blue tent." "Your muscles go after you're *burnt*, . . ." "Canadian sailors *burnt* in the North Atlantic . . ." ". . . crude oil *burning* all around them . . ." ". . . the *burning* ring of fire come to life . . ." "I can't re-call what happened when the *burnt* sailors moved back into the *non-burnt* world . . ." ". . . a nurse's uniform does something for *Burn Man*, for *Burn Man* is not *burnt* everywhere, still has desires . . ." "Some people from my old school . . . fried themselves over years and years, *burned* out over dissolute decades . . ." ". . . my *Burn Man* motorcycle . . ." "Before I became *Burn Man*, the Texas woman kissed me . . ." "*Burn Man* must have his face cov-ered . . ." "Perhaps my *Burn Man* skin is more accurate now . . ." "As a kid I was *burned* by the summer sun in Penticton." "Kids in pyjamas watched me *burn* like Guy Fawkes . . ." ". . . the *burnt* forest floor . . ." "No one new joins my *Burn Man* Club. *Burn Man* is alive . . ." "*Burn Man* climbs inside mask and clown suit like a scuba diver . . ." ". . . trying to enter the hide of *Burn Man's* teeming serious face . . ." And the last sentence of the story reads: "And a famous scuba diver rockets like a lost dark god into smoking stands of Douglas fir, into black chimneys *burning*."

Jarman also uses image patterning in a stricter sense. Cer-tain pictures, moments, or images repeat through the story. For example, the image of the porch on which the Texas woman kissed him: "Once, maybe, I was chosen, necking on the Hop-per porch, that stunning lean of a Texas woman into my arms . . ." ". . . my hunger and love for a porch . . ." "Before I became Burn Man, the Texas woman kissed me at the bottom of her lit yellow stairs, porch dark as tar. . . ." (The significant words here—Texas, porch, kiss, lit, yellow, and stairs—splinter out sub-patterns, e.g. ". . . sang their night code to me alone: Texas, kiss, lit stairs . . .") ". . . flame whispered in my ear, like a woman on a porch," ". . . my hunger and love for a porch . . ." "The woman on the Texas porch said . . ." ". . . a mysterious person falling toward me on a Texas porch with her tongue rearranging hope in my mouth." "Tristan falls in love on a Hopper porch . . ."

Another form of repetition Jarman uses, structural repetition, bears mentioning here. For example, Burn Man masquerades as a clown and a moose; Cindi, the escort, dresses up as a nurse. The act of masquerading connects Cindi and Burn Man: "All of us risk something, dress as something . . ." But Cindi dresses up as a nurse (". . . a slight woman in a parody of a nurse's uniform does something for Burn Man . . ." "My slight Nurse Wretched . . .") which makes her a double of the nurse in the burn ward (". . . the nurse with the honed Andalusian face tried not to touch me too hard." "The nurse with the determined Spanish face . . . her serious expression and unfucked-up skin and my hunger and love for a porch . . ."). What this curious doubling means is difficult to say, but the echo of the nurse in Cindi tends to deepen and complicate Burn Man's relationship with both women. It is also, quite simply, a form of embellishment, a way of making a text more lively and interesting in the sense used above. This kind of doubling creates connection and cohesion where, in real terms, little exists.

Jarman explicitly uses the word "double" when Burn Man splits from the I narrator. "At some point in this year of our Lord I began to refer to myself in the third person, as a double: Burn Man . . ." But Burn Man also finds a surprising double in the off-duty police man kicked to death in the bar ("In that instant, like me, he was changed, *his* memory jammed on a loop in a jar of wind, living the blues, dying." Note how the doubling is created by the use of a tie-in phrase "like me.") and the mysterious dead scuba diver found in a burned-out forest. The scuba diver gets introduced as a golf buddy's tall tale, then the doubling takes place at the story's close (". . . Burn Man climbs inside mask and clown suit like a scuba diver . . . And a famous scuba diver rockets like a lost dark god into smoking stands of Douglas fir, into black chimneys burning.") in a densely-woven matrix of tie-ins and associations. And, of course, "climbs inside mask and clown suit" reminds us of Cindi-the-escort-dressed-as-a-nurse, so that the story begins to implode in a way, everything means everything else, and the equations may end up meaning nothing at all beyond the pleasure of their own formal play.

This small collection of examples goes nowhere near exhausting the riot of verbal invention Jarman deploys in "Burn Man on a Texas Porch." But how to contextualize this riot? What does it mean? Of course, what drives a writer's hand always remains secret, sometimes even from himself. We surge toward the shapes we love without knowing why we love them. Jarman's taste is rhetorical—not just because he uses a lot of classical rhetorical devices, but also because his narratives are monologues, speeches. He harks back to an ancient tradition of eloquent speaking much despised, as Marshall McLuhan pointed out, by Plato, the logician, who saw no place for poets in his republic. This tradition of literary revel has come down to us through the Elizabethans and thence to Joyce and the Irish and also, somehow, to the American South. But always it has been in conflict with a counter-tradition of the plain style, of pure representation, of telling a story the good old-fashioned way without the author drawing attention to himself and his oral pyrotechnics. Jarman doesn't care for the plain style. He's intoxicated with words and the playful ways they can be strung together using sound and rhythm and repetition. And the meaning he is after is not the meaning of the didact or some mirror of the world, but a meaning that murmurs through the words of a text like wind in leaves and reveals itself mysteriously in the play of language itself.

MEMOIRS OF
THE UNDEAD

CEES NOOTEBOOM'S
THE FOLLOWING STORY

Heb. 11-4. . . . *he being dead yet speaketh.*

. . . suddenly in his expressions and looks the unforgettable emerges and imparts to everything that concerned him that authority which even the poorest wretch in dying possesses for the living around him. This authority is at the very source of the story. (Benjamin, Illuminations*)*

CEES NOOTEBOOM's novel *The Following Story* is a book about dead people from the point of view of a dead man. After you read the book, your first thought is, Who could have imagined dead people talked so much and had such interesting lives?

Nooteboom is Dutch and, thus, apt to see the comic side of dying. When a neighbour observes that his hero Herman Mussert looks dead when he's reading, Herman replies, "What you call dead, madame, is in fact concentration." Nooteboom writes out of a modern northern European tradition—grounded in post-Protestantism, Greek and Roman classics, and Celtic mythology: Herman resolutely claims not to believe in life after death; one of the characters might be Persephone, Queen of the Underworld; Plato offers the ultimate commentary on death and dying; and the Land of the Dead is somewhere in the West.

The Following Story was inspired by Ambrose Bierce's Civil War story "An Occurrence at Owl Creek Bridge"—the whole book eventuates in the two seconds or so it takes Herman to die one night in his Amsterdam apartment. One of the conventions of the novel of death, to coin a critical category, is that time deforms. This means that author can have a lot technical fun fooling around with narrative time; the distortion of chronology is thematically motivated by the conventional ways we talk about life, death, and time. When we die we go out of time (the normal time of clocks and calendars) and enter eternity—eternity is the same as no time or some paradoxically endless simultaneity. In Nooteboom's novel, time expands so that Herman Mussert can tell the story of important events in his life in the two seconds of his dying.

The Following Story is 115 pages long, divided roughly in the middle into two parts. In the first part, the protagonist Herman Mussert wakes up in a Lisbon hotel room despite having gone to bed the night before in his apartment in Amsterdam. He has "the ridiculous feeling that I might be dead," though he can't be certain. The Lisbon hotel room is familiar because, twenty years before, Herman spent a night there with his married lover Maria Zeinstra. At this point, the novel begins to proceed along a double narrative line: Herman recalls his affair with Maria and, at the same time, revisits, in the present, the Lisbon he and Maria once knew, testing the strangeness of his situation and his intuition about being dead. Nowadays, Herman is a mediocre travel writer, but twenty years before he was a classics teacher ("dead language teacher," as his students called him) in a Dutch private school where Maria and her husband also taught. Herman fell in love with Maria while observing a class she gave on "death"—most of which involved watching a film about a female sexton beetle mating and laying her eggs in a carrion pellet she fashions out of a dead rat. Meanwhile Maria's husband is having an affair with Herman's prize student Lisa d'India.

The second half the novel seems oddly disjointed at first. At the end of the first part, Herman is back at his hotel falling asleep in Lisbon, or possibly he is thrashing about in his sleep in Amsterdam. The second part opens with Herman describing his fellow passengers as they embark from Lisbon on a voyage across the Atlantic to Brazil. Gradually, the reader realizes that this is a death ship, a ferry to the Land of the Dead, that all the passengers are dead, or, perhaps more correctly, in the process of casting off the last vestiges of their lives on Earth. Accompanying them is a mysterious female "guide," and in the course of the journey each of the passengers tells the story of his death and then vanishes with the guide (who may or may not be Persephone but who looks, to Herman, like his student Lisa d'India). At the climactic moment, Herman tells the guide the story of how his love affair ended, his last great class, in which he performs Socrates' death scene from Plato's *Phaedo*, his ridiculous public scuffle with Maria's husband in the schoolyard afterwards, and Lisa d'India's subsequent death in a car accident as Maria's husband and she race away together. The book ends with Herman turning from the ship's rail to address his mysterious female guide and interlocutor. The last words are: "And then I told her, then I told you the following story." Thus, the novel becomes circular and unending.

Nooteboom's tone is urbane and intellectual, his vision of death ultimately consoling. He writes the absence, so to speak: he imagines the unimaginable, that is, what it might be like to die (and keep on talking). He invents a fictional world in which it is plausible for the dead to speak. This comes about despite the fact that the main character stubbornly insists that existence beyond death is impossible. Maria asks Herman, "Do you believe in an afterlife?"

> "No," I replied, truthfully. I am not even sure we exist at all, I wanted to say, and then I went and said it.

Which does not prevent him from stretching out his last seconds with memory, meditation, and action, filling the emptiness, as it were, with substance.

Nooteboom's novel, interestingly enough, is also a love story, which makes a certain structural sense: dead people don't want much and tend to fail to generate plot; plot has to eventuate from some other source. Herman's last act is to recall the ridiculous tragedy of his affair with Maria twenty years before, the first and only time he was ever in love.

It is suggestive to think of the story of Herman's death as a dramatic backdrop for the love-adultery plot, a warrant, in a way, for the significance of a tawdry little in-house affair between two school teachers, one already married. Or we might think of the death story as a dramatic occasion, or frame, a rhetorical flourish, that makes the telling of the story itself riveting. The real action of the narrative takes place in the past, the dead or dying recalling it for the reader. Thus the narrative setup itself has a kind of epic armature which lends power and significance to the story.

Death, in this aspect, is an aesthetic artifice, a way of setting up what the Russian Formalist Viktor Shklovsky called a "differential perception," a discrepancy from the norm that generates a frisson of excitement. Differential perception is closely related to the Formalist idea of enstrangement, the process by which artful form rescues experience from convention. In Nooteboom's novel, the experience rescued from conventional discourse by the unexpected point of view is Herman Mussert's tawdry little love affair (not a triangle but a quadrilateral: married couple, fellow teacher, and student) which, in the penumbral atmosphere of that Atlantic crossing, glitters with a desperate, lonely passion and tragic comedy.

The author's objective at the outset is to create a coherent system of ideas, repetitive structures, reminders and reflectors to establish a plausible novel world. This objective holds for any novel, but, in this case, the plausibility needs to be goosed because the events described are highly improbable, death being one of those experiences we all share but rarely get to report on (unlike, say, losing your virginity). To put it another way, the novel has to be made to appear plausibly implausible. Nooteboom manages to imply a basic narrative assumption: dead people don't normally tell stories, but for the sake of this book, they do. He manages this in a number of cunning ways.

Readers take their cues from characters. So authors pay attention to how their characters react to the premises of the story. As I've already mentioned, Herman Mussert in *The Following Story* doesn't believe in an afterlife. In fact, he doesn't quite believe he exists in the first place. When pressed by Maria, he espouses a sort of uber-rational, postmodern construction of the self as a "cluster of composite, endlessly altering circumstances and functions which we address as 'I'." He would be the last person to entertain ideas about the survival of the soul after the death of the body. And so there is a certain backhand confirmatory power when, on the very first page of the novel, Herman dryly entertains the possibility of his own demise.

> I had waked up with the ridiculous feeling that I might be dead, but whether I was actually dead, or had been dead, or vice versa, I could not ascertain.

Thus the question posed at the opening of the novel is not whether or not there is an afterlife but whether or not Herman is dead, a subtle but important shifting of the argument. Through the first half of the novel, Herman exhibits logic and curiosity in examining his own state of being or not being. And the reader then slides by easy (and, apparently, reasonable) stages toward the moment of Herman's final acceptance of his own continuity after or at least during the moment of death, a moment that he greets with stoical tranquility and anticipation. (As do all his fellow passengers on that westbound death ship—a boy, a priest, a salesman, a Chinese scholar, a commercial pilot.)

In a sense, Herman becomes a reader of his own book and we read him reading the other characters and his own reactions for clues as to his situation. This is especially true in the final half of the novel, the journey to the Land of the Dead on that transatlantic liner with no name (operated by "an old ferryman"). The reader sides with Herman and composes the world of the novel through his reading of experience. And the second half of the novel, with its multiple rehearsals of death through the deaths of Herman's fellow passengers ("we the travelers in limbo"), sets the rules and context for what is to happen to Herman himself. He observes the strangely courteous camaraderie of the passengers, he watches their private colloquies with the mysterious female guide, he listens as one by one they begin to shun daylight, start to evanesce, tell the stories of their deaths and then disappear into the darkness.

> . . . we died each other's deaths; we helped each other to stretch that final second to last until the end of each story . . .

This terminal story-hour recurs five times, five different deaths endured by five characters (call these parallel plots or

congruent subplots—rhyme at the level of action) before it is
Herman's turn, and by then the reader is ready, fully versed in
the ceremonies of departure which are at the heart of this novel.

Authors use repetitive actions—scene, plot and subplot—to "force"
(call it thematic encoding or stamping, as if the text is rubber-stamped
all over with the same words) their agenda on the novel and construct
a focus of concern. I use the word "force" to connote a special kind
of obsessiveness authors exhibit when they aim for aesthetic
and thematic coherence. It is an obsessiveness that goes beyond
what seems realistic; paradoxically, the effect of obsessiveness in
a text is to reinforce narrative plausibility.

In this case, the book is about death. So actual deaths and
death words are ubiquitous. This one might expect given that
most of the characters in the novel in question are dead. But
Nooteboom is insistent. The words "death" and "dead" appear
five times on the first page of *The Following Story*. When
Herman comes to describe himself as a teacher, he reminds us
that the students call him a "dead language teacher," with the
ironic dangling modifier. I have earlier mentioned the joke
about the neighbour who thinks he looks dead when in fact he's
reading.

After a while, everything in *The Following Story* seems to
refer to or remind the narrator of death, from the "dead dust" at
his feet to his own "deathly quiet" or the "deathly quiet" of the
wrestling match between Thisbe and Peleus. When he thinks
of his beloved unfinished and ongoing Ovid translation, he
remembers the bit about the dead Achilles—". . . scarce enough
to fill an urn. . . ," then tells us that if he is "to be interred in a
grave," he will take the translation with him. Observing that his
Lisbon hotel is hard by the Tagus River, he remembers an apt
quotation from the Dutch poet Slauerhoff: "Within my being
I'm decaying, I know now the cause of my dying, on the banks of
the Tagus' flow, where life is light and slow." This is a sure sign

of forcing: when an author chooses a thematically apt epithet (or quotation) instead of going for mere local colour. (Passages of mere local colour are signs of second-rate writing.)

Nooteboom, of course, deploys an obligatory death scene. Herman Mussert is dying, in a manner of speaking, throughout the novel. And his actual death in bed in Amsterdam is mostly skirted in the text save for a single climactic moment at the end of the first half of the novel. Note the tell-tale splitting of Herman's self, the subtle transformation of I to he.

> I saw myself lying in bed in Amsterdam. I slept, tossing and turning my head, and crying, still clutching the photograph from the evening newspaper in my left hand. I looked at the little Japanese alarm clock I always kept next to my bed. What sort of time can this be in which time stands still? It wasn't any later than it had been when I went to sleep. The dark shape at my feet had to be Night Owl, successor to Bat. I could see that the man in Amsterdam wanted to wake up, he was thrashing about, his right hand groped for his glasses, but it was not he who switched on the light; it was me, here in Lisbon.

This "thrashing" moment is preceded by a run-up, a series of metaphorical death experiences, the mysterious, over-whelming, and uncanny experience of death here represented repeatedly as a wave and artfully woven into narrative, a kind of rhythmic textual pulse or bass note (italics for clarity).

> I noticed that I was getting drowsy, and at the same time it was as if a *great wave* swept me up, lifting me, engulfing me, carrying me along with a force that I did not know existed. I thought of death, but . . .

It struck me that the thought preoccupying me, whatever it was, had been trying desperately to attune itself to the slow *wave* that seemed bearing me along.

The *wave* that had overwhelmed me in my sleep of half-sleep had been fear, physical fear that I would fall off the earth which hung there, so detached and unprotected in space.

How long I slept I do not know, but again it seemed as if an unspeakable force was tugging at me, that I was borne along by a current against which a poor swimmer such as myself was powerless, that an enormous, all-encompassing *wave* slapped me down on a deserted beach.

These passages are reinforced elsewhere in the phrasing—"the sweet black liquid of death" and the "liquid I."

Beyond Herman Mussert's own experience of death, Nooteboom invents ways of putting death into every scene, so that over and over the plot circles back to death. Herman falls in love with Maria when he audits her high-school biology class on animal death—a gorgeously comic scene involving a film of a female sexton beetle rolling a dead rat ("It wasn't a big rat, but it was extremely dead . . .") into a carrion pellet, mating with her lover, laying her eggs in the rotting rat and then vomiting on it to tenderize it for her offspring.

This woman was teaching me new words! There was no doubt about it, I loved her.

"In two days' time she will lay her eggs there. But first she is going to tenderize the carrion."

Her eggs! I had never seen a beetle vomit before. I was sitting in the classroom with the woman I loved. . . .

In a mirroring scene, Maria audits Herman's class on the death of Phaethon—who flies too near the sun and perishes—after which they have some flirtatious dialogue about cremation. Here the forcing of theme onto scene results in both scenes becoming set-piece paradigms of the whole book, melding sex, death, and transformation. This creates a structural tightness and focus and, yes, plausibility that reinforces the organic unity of the novel and adds a lovely echo effect.

Yet a third great death scene (since, as Herman observes, "everything has to rhyme in my life"—self-reference lurks throughout; great novels are always commenting on their own structure) occurs at the end of the novel, just prior to the climax of the Maria-Herman love crack-up. In this scene, Herman re-enacts for his class the death of Socrates from Plato's *Phaedo*, his end-of-term tour de force. (One of Herman's multiple nicknames is Socrates so that in enacting the death of Socrates he is rehearsing his own death.) "Now I am about to die. I gaze into the eyes of my pupils just as he must have gazed into the eyes of his." And then, of course, someone really does die—Herman's student Lisa d'India (who re-appears to him on the death ship as his guide, his Persephone) trapped in a runaway car with her idiotic basketball coach-poet-lover.

I have already mentioned the five fellow passengers on the death ship and their last stories as examples of parallel actions. But there is a pre-plot formation, a memory scene, set near the beginning of the novel where Herman recalls a trip to the Space Museum in Washington some years before. The memory is triggered by a newspaper photograph of the spaceship Voyageur; Herman recalls seeing an exhibit about Voyageur and the tears he shed imagining that man-made object shooting out of the solar system, past dead cold planets. The image of Voyageur is an image of the soul churning away from earth, an image of death, which staggers Herman. And he's holding the photograph of the spacecraft when he dies in his Amsterdam bed. The Voyageur memory also introduces the notion of death as a journey which is picked up and reiterated in the Socrates' death scene and at the very close of the novel (Herman Mussert, of course, is a travel writer).

Authors use repeated images, words and concepts to reinforce the thematic encoding of a text.

Nooteboom creates recursive patterns which are mostly about words or ideas, not precisely image patterns, which by association continue to force the death theme even when the narrator seems to be wandering away from the topic. For example, there are multiple animadversions on time (not to mention clocks). This stands to reason because, as mentioned above, the difference between life, which occurs in time, and the eternity of death, which is timeless, is a crucial logical distinction between the living and the dead. So there is the strange "Hora Legal" clock with its stern admonition ". . . mine is the only true time, the durable now encompassing sixty counted seconds" to which Herman responds with the thought:

> Clocks served two purposes, in my opinion. The first was to tell people the time, and the second to impress upon me that time is an enigma, an intractable measureless phenomenon into which, out of sheer helplessness, we have introduced a semblance of order.

A page later he playfully introduces his illicit lover Maria Zeinstra to a clock in a Lisbon bar that only tells the right time if you look at it in a mirror. And then there is the "little Japanese alarm clock I always keep next to my bed" which stops while he is sleeping. "What sort of time can this be in which time stands still?"

In the second half of the novel, we are in the spirit realm and time exists or not in multiple ways. Time either stretches, or slows down, as it were ("we helped each other to stretch that final second"). Or it speeds up—one of the travelers, a Chinese scholar-poet, observes: "For our spirits—and for yours, too, I presume?—that time passes much more quickly than ordinary time." Or it recurs. Another passenger tells Herman: "I have always admired the Portuguese for this—you depart from Belem, you arrive in Belem. There's something cyclical about it, something of eternal recurrence. Not that you believe in that sort of thing, or do you?" To which Herman dryly replies, "Only in the case of animals." The concept of eternal recurrence is reinforced by the way the novel ends, the last words returning us to the beginning of the text.

Change is another pattern forced into the text of *The Following Story*. In that amazing comic set-piece death-class with the female sexton beetle and her dead rat, Nooteboom makes an explicit connection between death and metamorphosis.

> . . . her lesson was not so much about death as about what comes after, about metamorphosis. And although hers was a different order than mine, the subject of metamorphosis was familiar to me.

The word "metamorphosis" and the theme of change has already appeared in the novel at this point because, of course, Herman is working on a translation of Ovid's *Metamorphoses*. And he's teaching a class on Ovid, which is the one Maria audits, the class on Phaethon's death. Herman says to her, "Why don't you join my Ovid class. I'll be dealing with change, too. Not rats into pellets of carrion, but still. . . ." But at this point change is firmly established as a branch of the main death pattern and recurs throughout.

> *Ignis mutat res*, I muttered, but *my* matter was not to be changed by any fire. I had already changed . . .

There was nothing to prove it, but they had changed—
no; they had changed *again*. Things were disappearing,
lines were missing.

In the last pages of the novel, Nooteboom returns to this
motif when Herman meditates on the disintegration of his body
after he is dead.

> . . . at the same time I would change. It was not my soul
> that would set out on a journey, as the real Socrates had
> imagined; it was my body that would embark on endless
> wanderings, never to be ousted from the universe, and so
> it would take part in the most fantastic metamorphoses,
> about which it would tell me nothing because it would
> long since have forgotten all about me.

There is some lesson here about the way novels are constructed
but also the way our so-called reality is constructed, that is,
the profoundly human way we have of weaving reality out of
words which are like purses with holes in the bottom. We keep
putting the money or meaning in and it keeps falling out.

To put this another way, a plausible fictional universe implies
the possibility of a fictional plausible universe. The structures
which lend plausibility, focus and meaningful density to a piece
of writing are primarily structures of repetition and it is by
repetition that we know the so-called reality we inhabit, that is,
we know that reality through our ability to apply consistent and
predictable descriptions to it.

Death frames and authenticates the story of Herman
Mussert's love affair; its stamped imprint is everywhere in the
novel; the characters move in a World of Death. It is as if the
author wished to give the reader a world braided with reminders

of death, with that consciousness of eternity that brushes us so rarely these days at funerals, death beds, and hospice wards. The novel is a *memento mori*, an intimation of mortality.

Herman Mussert is a good man who loves books, who pursues his unremunerative translation work for love, and who loves just one woman (albeit his love object is an impolitic choice). Steeped in the classics, the tradition of the epic, he steps into his classroom in the guise of Socrates and enacts, in the manner of the ancient storytellers, the greatest death scene ever written. Only one student responds to the moral invitation, and she is already marked out for death herself. She writes him a note, a message lost in the novel when Herman's lover tells him to rip it up unread.

Of course, all this being said, we know nothing more about death than we did when we began this novel. Not only is it a novel and, hence, not real, but death itself is at best a notional concept, something mostly experienced, as I have said, from the outside. Real death remains an impenetrable mystery. It is a null concept, a lapse, a fissure. But I am reminded here of Walter Benjamin's essay on the Russian story writer Leskov in which Benjamin writes: "Death is the sanction of everything that the storyteller can tell. He has borrowed his authority from death."

NOVELS AND DREAMS

LEON ROOKE'S
A GOOD BABY

THE BEST NOVELS are like dreams. They come out of the silence of the page like a dream. They structure themselves like dreams; that is, there are clear ways in which the structure of dreams parallels the structure of novels. Like dreams, novels use image patterning as a device for suggesting meaning: image repetition, association, juxtaposition, and splintering (Viktor Shklovsky's term for the branching pattern created by a repeating image and its associated or split-off elements, which also repeat). Like dreams, novels are available to interpretation; the best novels have a central luminous mystery at their core which tempts generations upon generations of critics and readers to find new structures and meanings beyond the surface of the words. And like dreams, novels are built around (and this is explicable in only the vaguest of terms) the recurrence or insistence of desire which, in order to generate plot, must be resisted; the locus or arena of desire and resistance appears again and again with obsessive regularity in novels, an obsessive regularity which, in real life, would seem eccentric if not pathological. In novels, character is perversion, and the novel returns again and again to the animating desire which it must resist to the bitter end or even beyond the end of the words on the page.

Leon Rooke's novel *A Good Baby* bears the epigraph: "Whereon do you lead me, bright rider?" This epigraph has always puzzled me because, to begin with, there aren't any bright riders in the book. About three-quarters of the way through *A Good Baby*, there is an extremely strange chapter in the point of view of the baby's aunt, a girl who has spent most of the novel trudging through the eerie landscape of Rooke's imagination trying to catch up with her sister Lena and Lena's murderous lover Truman. In the chapter in question, this sister awakes from a trance-like sleep and encounters a blind man on a horse. This blind man has appeared to her once before and in that instance he was leading a mule which never followed the same road twice except on its return journey. If you think about it, this blind man seems like an emissary of death, or he is Death. He just appears, takes the sister to Lena's body, then drops out of the book. This blind man on a horse is the only rider in the novel and this chapter begins with an italicized paragraph: "*Whip me along, bright rider. Whip me along, O my caretaker, like you done in my dream-house hour.*" A paragraph later, there is another italicized passage: "*Hit and bleed me, dark runner. Cozen and devour us here among your dwarf-elders.*" Bright rider and dark runner are here syntactically parallel and thus identical. But these two italicized passages seem somehow to emerge out of the page on their own without conventional textual support. No one says these lines; no one thinks them; they are not attached to the narrative in any other way. In a sense they parallel the emergence of the blind horseman who in his first appearance materialized "out of the mist," "a ghostly mist."

We here enter the dreamlike core of Rooke's novel, the place where the planks of conventional narrative prose drop out from under the reader, and words take on a puzzling yet insistent significance and characters do not so much act as surface into the narrative as though driven by some hidden necessity. The novel starts by transporting its actors into this foggy environment. After Lena and Truman have sex and visit the bootlegger in the first chapter, they drive deeper and deeper into the hills, crossing county lines. Lena says, "I never bin up to this country . . . Folks my way says they's backwards up here, though fierce, and loyal to the dog." Truman wonders: "this land he'd ventured into was so switch-backed, so witchified to its cones and to its depths." It is a place where even the civil and temporal powers signified by the certainty of the daily mail have lost their sure grip—"Mail did git thue once in a blue moon." And Rooke makes much of "the abiding haze of fog which marked their passage." All of which reminds me of other mythic journeys to the Land of the Dead, that peculiar mirror Other Place where everything we hold familiar is inverted and strange. I think here of Marlow's halting, fog-shrouded journey up that distant African river in "Heart of Darkness." "What we could see was just the steamer we were on, her outlines blurred as though she had been on the point of dissolving, and a misty strip of water, perhaps two feet broad, around her—and that was all. The rest of the world was nowhere. . . ." In both passages, the Rooke page with the bright rider reference and Conrad's fog sequence, the word "trance" appears, as though the fog were a physical manifestation of the mental state occasioned by a journey which crosses, not geographical, but metaphysical borders. And in turn this narrative journey into the fog of trance and dream implies a form that is vague, mysterious and inscrutable. Here again, a passage I adore from "Heart of Darkness": "But Marlow was not typical (if this propensity to spin yarns be excepted), and to him the meaning of an episode was not inside like a kernel but outside, enveloping the tale which brought it out only as a glow brings out a haze, in the likeness of one of these misty halos that sometimes are made visible by the spectral illumination of moonshine."

We speak here of stories that make some metaphoric leap and limn a journey that is not outward but reaches some dark innerscape where meaning is obscure yet luminous. It quickly becomes apparent to the reader of *A Good Baby* that the baby itself is more than a baby. Even Truman, the baby's father, who later murders its mother, recalls the luminousness of its conception. ". . . that time with the hat, he'd seen some special light in her face he'd never seen in no female's face before, hat or otherwise, and it was some kind of radiance afloat there. It tickled him, that radiance." This radiance is transferred in the course of the novel to the baby itself. "That baby. Its skin glows some in the dark, don't it? Unhuh. This here's a special baby." This is about all the baby does in the course of the novel, but in relation to plot, the baby becomes the universal object of desire, the empty yet radiant sign to which every human is drawn.

I like to say when I teach that the novel is a machine of desire; that is, the novel is a form that presupposes desire as the engine of plot. The reason we like to read good novels is not because we identify with this or that character's particular desire; it is because we identify with any desire and any character who desires. The novel incarnates a universal plot which reads something like Freud's clash between the Pleasure Principle and the Reality Principle. You know how this goes: infants begin life with no sense of separation between themselves and the world. What they wish for they receive. But the process of maturation involves the gradual separation of self from the world, the gradual realization that there is a gap between what we want and the getting of it. This radical disconnect is the universal plot: we want and we can't have. The mother withdraws the breast; the world resists desire. Every novel is an adventure of thwarted megalomania, the nuzzling infant searching for the retreating yet radiant object of desire. Desire then leads us into strange places, and in the end it desires only the end to desiring which is death.

A Good Baby is really about a kind of dream inversion of the story of the runaway breast; the baby, in this case, becomes not itself but what everyone desires, a magical love fetish that will heal the sick at heart, replace ancient losses and satisfy the crude and brittle lusts of old men. Comically enough, the baby is indestructible (like the dream of a breast); Toker, the hero of the novel, drags it around in a bag, feeds it on soda, rarely cleans it, yet the baby remains docile, healthy and radiant. Toker doesn't even want the baby—in this novel, those who don't want find love and those who want find only disappointment and ashes. Toker starts out the novel in the Western equivalent of Hindu abandonment. His horrendous childhood has blasted his desire mechanism to bits. He lives hermit-like in the smoky ruins of his burned-out family home, remembering over and over the day his mother killed his dog, burned his sister to death and left town. Released from wanting (though he lusts after a woman he calls Roby, we find out later in the novel that he's a virgin), he dwells in his own Land of the Dead only to find the good baby under a laurel bush and be healed. He keeps trying to give the baby away, keeps telling the baby that "he wont its mother" until in a strange and mysterious scene with Sarah, the invalid wife of the general store owner, he actually learns to "talk" like a woman. "She studied the answer, then said, Yes, yes. I can see another woman might have said that. Now try again. Say somethin else. The sort of thing a woman would." The plot of the novel is built on the curious convergence and recurrence of everyone else's desire for the baby and Toker's desire to get rid of the baby which magically transforms as he undergoes his own dream gender change and becomes a mother. "I can see you held that baby long enough, you'd holder how a woman would," says Sarah, the store-owner's wife.

There is an odd, dreamlike purity to Toker's desire to get rid of the baby and everyone else's desire for the baby. In Rooke's novel, there is hardly anything like conventional characterization. Every person in the novel exists along a single line of loss and desire. Sometimes they're sly about how they pitch their desires, and sometimes they are clearly mad. But that is about the limit of variation. And there is nothing in this novel like a nod to conventional psychological paradigms of character development. Toker's obliterated childhood, his wound, is more mythic than psychological. It leaves him not corrupted but somehow cauterized, burned down to a nub of innocent simplicity. "I do believe," says Sarah, "that in every respect you're nearabouts as innocent as that baby."

Toker's dark double, his evil twin, Truman, is the baby's father, its mother's murderer. Truman is desire incarnate, a shambling beast of desire who lurches awkwardly through the novel trying over and over again to re-enact scenes from his childhood. It is Truman who gets to announce what I take to be the novel's surface moral: ". . . they's so much dereliction in the need of things." He is a classic fetishist. Needing to relive the ur-scene of his first sexual humiliation—a brilliant Rookean parody of Humbert Humbert's first love in *Lolita*—he places a crude child's hair bow on Lena's head, a bow like the one worn by Patience, the girl who taunted him and fought him off in his youth. Truman's desires insist; they recur; they drive him into mechanical and ritualized repetitions so monomaniacal and maladroit that they are doomed to comic failure. Living inside a fetishized (dream) universe, Truman is blind to any portion of reality that might help him achieve even one of his desires: to kiss Patience, to trap a mink (surely, in part, a dream conversion of the word "minx," hence Patience again; "his mind crawling backwards *to that time of the mink, when she . . .*"), and to retrieve the baby for his own evil purposes. "What's mine is mine. That trap is mine, and that baby is mine. I'll go and gitter."

A Good Baby, like a dream, is a metonymic (read fetishized) world of desire. The plot is barely a plot, less a plot than the simple reiteration of desire. Toker wanders around with the baby trying to find someone to take it while fending off every person who actually wants the baby. Truman bumps along the backroads in his disintegrating car, never getting close enough to do any damage until the final chapter when the dreamlike fog which attends the whole novel suddenly seems to condense into a deus ex machina flood (how this brings back memories of *Mill on the Floss*) that swooshes Truman out of the book. Truman does not, however, die; it does not escape me that this is a dream-trip down the birth canal and into some other world.

But, finally, a novel is not a dream; novels and dreams only share common structures. Novels need to deal with time in a way completely alien to the world of dream. And novels need to offer their readers at least a superficial plausibility or verisimilitude. Even the strangest novels never completely untether themselves from allegiance to a certain commonsense conception of reality which is at once familiar and artificial. Again, "Heart of Darkness" is instructive. Marlow makes his mythic dream journey upriver through the fog into the heart of darkness. After Kurtz dies, Marlow himself narrowly escapes death. He has looked, as he says, into the abyss. When he returns to the white city of Brussels, the sepulchral center of imperial capitalism, and meets Kurtz's Intended, rather than tell the truth, he serves up a beautiful and comforting lie. We can journey into the world of dream, the universe of death, Marlow is telling us, but we cannot tell the truth when we return. The mystery must forever remain a mystery lest the day to day fabric of social discourse be forever torn asunder. The traveler can only speak in lies or parables; he can tell stories which radiate a meaning beyond meaning, hinting at what he saw. The beautiful lie Marlow tells sometimes seems like the most terrifying moment in the story.

Rooke's *A Good Baby* proposes a different sort of ending, a kind of neo-Christian redemptive closure, based on the capture of that errant breast-object, the glowing baby. "Jiggers, a baby! the brother declared. A baby will save the world!" Instead of bringing his novel back from the mist-circled hill country, the realm of dream, death and myth, Rooke ejects evil and leaves us in a reconstituted world of gratified desire. He even stage-manages a resurrection of the nuclear family—Roby and Toker cuddling in bed with the baby between them after wonderful sex—when every family in the novel till that moment has been exploded, wracked with loss, or rendered sterile (one insistent recurring motif is the story of the lost child). It is as if, in finding the baby, Toker has won the metaphysical lottery; this brings an amused smile to our lips as does that vision of Truman as a comic book Satan, a bumbling, Keystone imp of Hell. Here dream has become fantasy; it has become mere wish fulfillment; it has become the comforting lie (and I suppose it is true that all dreams are not nightmares).

In this regard, I think *A Good Baby* is a bit at war with itself. I think Rooke's larger allegiance is to the dark side, to the thumping reiteration of desire, to the desolation of loss and the immense carelessness of need. Like Marlow, Truman pities and condescends to women. "They were that fragile in their wanting," he thinks. But here women stand in, as a symbol, for hearth and home, for the system of domestic virtues and customs which form the fabric of civilization. "They were that fragile in their wanting" is finally a judgement on us all for we are all ultimately to be pitied for the endlessness of our desire. Kurtz and Marlow see that the end of desire is not gratification but death. This is the truth that cannot be told. That Rooke avoids this truth at the end of his novel does not prevent us from seeing that he lavishes his fiercest eloquence, his most haunting prose, his most insistent patterns, on the enigma of desire, on elegies of loss.

And so I come back to that puzzling epigraph: "Whereon do you lead me, bright rider?" and its companion passage: *"Whip me along, bright rider. Whip me along, O my caretaker, like you done in my dream-house hour."* This kind of heightened rhetoric belongs largely in the mind of Truman throughout. Truman is the one character who meditates on a "caretaker." And there is a pattern of italicized passages that insert themselves willy-nilly at the heads of chapters where otherwise they have no place—as if Truman's endless rant, his tent-preacher-from-Hell yammer, is invading and colonizing the rest of the novel. But is this really Truman thinking, or any other character in the novel, for that matter? Or are these moments rather the dreamlike emergence of some deeper pattern or interest? What is the dream-hour? Who is the bright rider (dark runner) and whither does he lead us (whip us on)?

I teach my writing students that in a formally correct narrative there are spaces, rhythmic pauses in the action, for what I call thematic passages. These are moments when the text itself seems to slow and gather itself, sifting the past for clues, casting forward for a track into the future of the book. At these moments, the novelist, as composer of the action, can come very close to the surface of his own text. I don't mean the nowadays diminished device of the authorial intrusion, the textual moment when the voice of the authority weighs into the narrative to guide the reader. I mean it in a more interrogative sense. There are moments all the way through the composition of a story or a novel when the author asks himself, Where am I going? What is this story about? What do my characters want? What is the meaning of this strange and beautiful thing I am inventing? It is very easy, I tell my students, to transfer these authorial meditations into the mind of a protagonist. In the interrogative mode, when they are all wondering about the nature of the universe in the midst of being enacted on the page, character, author and, yes, reader become one. And the novel becomes at once most real and most dreamlike.

These are the moments when the author comes closest to exhibiting his own struggle to form the fugitive elements of dream that inspire him into a narrative structure. But they are also the moments when the author comes closest to revealing the sources of his own animation, the compulsive sifting and tracking of those elements of dream whose whispered and fragmentary message is like the sound of distant music. In the midst of telling us how he found Kurtz, Marlow breaks off and says, "He was alone, and I before him did not know whether I stood on the ground or floated in the air. I've been telling you [you, here, being Marlow's friends on the Nellie, anchored in the Thames] what we said—repeating the phrases we pronounced— but what's the good? They were common everyday words—the familiar, vague sounds exchanged on every waking day of life. But what of that? They had behind them, to my mind, the terrific suggestiveness of words heard in dreams, of phrases spoken in nightmares."

We all know the murmured invitations of desire which lead us through life. But it seems to me that authors are more preternaturally haunted by the emptiness of desire, by the invisible constraints of form, by the endless whiteness of the page, and by the endlessness of need as it attaches itself to an infinite series of radiant objects. "Whereon do you lead me, bright rider?" reads the epigraph. "They were that fragile in their wanting," thinks Truman. "*Whip me along, bright rider. Whip me along. . . .*" These words are full of wonder, pity and compulsion. It is possible that in these mysterious passages in *A Good Baby* Leon Rooke is talking to himself about himself and about his dream which must appear to him, in this narrative guise, as a shining stranger, leading him, riding him, whipping him, into fog-shrouded mystery of his novel.

A SCRUPULOUS FIDELITY

THOMAS BERNHARD'S
THE LOSER

The Man and His Books

THOMAS BERNHARD IS DEAD. He had a terrible life, at least the early part. He was born in Holland where his Austrian mother had fled to escape the shame of her unwanted pregnancy. He never knew his father who died far away and in obscurity (and obscure circumstances). His mother mistreated him because of the shame he represented. Back in Austria he wanted to be an opera singer and studied music but caught a cold working at a menial job to make ends meet; the cold turned into tuberculosis. He was hospitalized repeatedly, his treatment was bungled, he was given up for dead, and survived just to prove how stupid his doctors were. Since opera-singing was out, he became a writer. He became a famous writer of deadpan, mordant, hilarious, difficult (modernist) novels and plays that often portray depressed characters with lung diseases.

Another common theme is Bernhard's disgust with his native Austria which he continually berated for its Nazi past, its stupidity, sentimentality, and philistinism. In his will he stipulated that none of his works could ever be published in Austria. Paradoxically he rarely left Austria and lived quietly in a country retreat outside of Vienna (many of his characters live in country retreats outside of Vienna).

Despite the fact that he seemed to put himself in every one of his novels, little is known about his intimate life. He wrote a five-volume memoir, *Gathering Evidence*, which is quite beautiful but, as all memoirs are, unrevealing. His first biographer somehow managed to discover that he liked to masturbate while watching himself in the mirror. This is both comic and significant; over and over Bernhard presents his narrators as characters watching themselves *think* about themselves. In fact, his narrators seem more interested in watching themselves *think* about themselves than in telling the story which often seems, upon analysis, more of an occasion for baroque invention than an end in itself. Reading Bernhard one is often reminded of the American experimentalist John Hawkes who once famously said:

> My novels are not highly plotted, but certainly they're elaborately structured. I began to write fiction on the assumption that the true enemies of the novel were plot, character, setting, and theme . . . structure—verbal and psychological coherence—is still my largest concern as a writer. Related or corresponding event, recurring image and recurring action, these constitute the essential substance or meaningful density of my writing. (*Wisconsin Studies in Contemporary Literature*, 1965)

Bernhard's narrators contradict themselves, digress, fall into hyperbolic rants that go on for pages, repeat themselves, and obsess, trapped, as it were, in a logorrheic paralysis. He writes whole books in one paragraph, eschews quotation marks, doesn't

mind run-on sentences, changes tense without reason, and ital-
icizes words apparently at random. Above all he is ironic, and
the reader can never be sure whether Bernhard means what he
says or is joking around. And, paradoxically, when he is just joking around, he is also being deadly serious. This is very puzzling to the reader accustomed to contemporary market-based
sentimental realism (make no mistake: we are in a Tea Party Lit
trough these days, driven by politics, recession and the cultural
terror inspired by the digital revolution), the kind of fiction
that tells a story about real characters we can identify with and
scenes we can recognize, the kind of novel North Americans
have come to expect, and, when they write, to write. In contrast
Bernhard's characters are almost all clownishly self-obsessed,
suicidal artists with lung diseases who cannot seem to tell a story
straight.

The Recession of Narrators

Thomas Bernhard's novel *The Loser* is the story of three aspiring concert pianists—Glenn Gould (drawn from real life), an
Austrian pianist named Wertheimer (the notional protagonist) and the unnamed narrator—who become friends in 1953
in Salzburg while studying piano with the great Horowitz.
Wertheimer and the narrator have dedicated their lives to becoming piano virtuosos, but one day they chance to overhear
Gould playing Bach's *Goldberg Variations* and his genius destroys them. Gould gracelessly adds insult to injury by calling
Wertheimer a loser; Wertheimer is the loser of the novel's title.

The narrator abandons the piano almost immediately; eventually he ends up living in Madrid writing a book called *About
Glenn* (which he periodically destroys and starts again). But
Wertheimer has a much more torturous unravelling. For years
he keeps playing, unable to abandon his dream. Finally he sells

his beloved Steinway and begins writing a book he also keeps destroying and re-starting; this book is called, yes, *The Loser*. At the same time he works off his disappointment in an abusive, quasi-incestuous relationship with his sister (the whole novel has Poe-ish overtones). Somehow the sister manages to escape Wertheimer's clutches, marrying a wealthy Swiss industrialist. Shortly after hearing that Glenn Gould has died suddenly of a stroke at the young age of 51, Wertheimer takes a train to Switzerland and hangs himself in front of his sister's house.

This is the skeletal story, the novel's bones, all told as thoughts and memories (not present-time forward-moving plot) through the point of view of the overwrought narrator who is, yes, writing about himself *thinking* about himself, the other characters, and the story of the novel in a farrago of anecdote, rant, digression, repetition, aphorism, and paradox *while also* planning to destroy the book he is writing—in a sense the book you are reading doesn't even exist.

> . . . today I write down this nonsense which I dare tell myself is *essayistic*, to use this hated word once again on my way to self-destruction, I write down these essayistic remarks, which in the end I will have to curse and tear up and thus destroy, and not a single person knows anymore that I myself once played the Goldberg Variations, though not as well as Glenn Gould. . . .

All the while, nothing happens: for the first 115 pages of the 170-page novel, the narrator describes himself standing alone in the front room of an inn *thinking*. Bernhard emphasizes the narrator's act of thinking-and-not-acting (logorrheic paralysis as a metonym for existential paralysis; the word "paralyzed" recurs relentlessly throughout the novel) to the point of self-parody:

The Steinway, **I thought while standing in the inn and looking about**, was aimed against my family.

Glenn's death had hit him *very hard*, he said, **I thought while standing in the inn.**

That certainly wasn't correct, **I thought now in the inn.**

[This is the end of the 115-page scene and the beginning of the next scene. The comma splice is the author's and is typical of his run-on dramatic transitions.] The so-called bottom line is *he* killed himself, not *I*, **I thought, I was just picking up my suitcase from the floor to put it on the bench, when the innkeeper walked in.** (115)

The narrator has actually come to the inn on a whim, out of curiosity, at least that's how he describes it at first. The notional present-time plot of the novel presents the narrator *thinking* about the main plot, the past, in the hours following Wertheimer's hasty funeral in Switzerland. Traveling back to Vienna from the funeral, the narrator has made an impulsive decision to get off the train at a rural station near Traich, Wertheimer's hunting lodge. He wants to search through Wertheimer's papers before the sister or anyone else conceals or destroys them, believing that those papers hold some secret about Glenn Gould that he can use in his own book. But later in the novel the narrator reveals a more sinister and damning reason for his quest.

If a friend dies we nail him to his own sayings, his comments, kill him with his own weapons . . . We exploit his unpublished papers in order to destroy even more the one who left them to us . . . We plunder everything that can be used against him in order to improve our situation.

The first 115 pages of the text, as I say, present the narrator alone in the inn. The next 30 pages present various conversations with the innkeeper (she was Wertheimer's lover), including some details of an undignified and uncharacteristic flood of parasitic guests at Traich just prior to the suicide. Then it takes 14 pages for the narrator to walk from the inn to Traich. And finally the last 13 pages of the novel take place at Traich, the narrator in conversation with Franz, the woodsman, who tells the story of Wertheimer's final weeks: Wertheimer, the loner, had a piano delivered from Vienna and invited a crowd of "artists" to come and stay; then he proceeded to drive them out of the house with his incessant, incompetent piano-playing; they destroyed his furniture, drank his booze, and then he finally paid for taxis to take them back to Vienna.

In the last lines of the book the narrator asks Franz for some time alone in Wertheimer's room. The papers and notes have all been burned (Wertheimer and Franz did this together); what remains is Gould's famous recording of the *Goldberg Variations*, still on the turntable where Wertheimer had left it when he went off to kill himself.

Thus before we even get to the details of Bernhard's rhetorical pyrotechnics we discover an immense amount of action on the structural level. There are, to begin with, three representational tempos: 1) the narrator writing the book which he ultimately expects to destroy; 2) the notional present which comprises most of the text, the narrator thinking as he waits in the inn, talks to the innkeeper and visits Traich; and 3) the recollected narrative of Wertheimer's *manie de perfection* and its comic-tragic aftermath. This technique of the receding point of view is not uncommon; Joseph Conrad uses a variant in "Heart of Darkness" as does Cervantes in *Don Quixote*; it parodies the naïve point of view structure commonly deployed in so-called realistic novels and ironizes the concept of point of view in gen-

eral—it is the literary version of the philosophical paradox of
the subject that cannot be an object to itself.

Stressed Form and the Duplication of Plot

Superimposed on this temporal grid are at least three plots:
1) the surface plot of the narrator's ultimately failed quest for
Wertheimer's papers at Traich—this plot being the occasion or
the pretext for the narrator's *re-thinking* of the past; 2) the main
plot, beginning 28 years earlier, in which Glenn Gould's genius
crushes Wertheimer's desire to be a "piano artist" and drives
him to his eventual suicide; and 3) what I call the shadow plot,
the vindictive story of the narrator's own disintegration and
his passive-aggressive role in Wertheimer's death revealed as a
Lacanian excess in his transparent snobbery, denial, self-justifi-
cation, and outrageous tirades.

> As always I was exaggerating now too, and to my own
> mind it was disturbing to suddenly hear myself call
> Wertheimer the tormentor and destroyer of his sister, I
> thought, I always behave this way with others, unjustly,
> even criminally.

You can imagine main plot and the shadow plot as two congruent triangles: Gould thwarts Wertheimer, and Wertheimer
deflects his animus onto his innocent sister (scapegoating is
a common theme in Bernhard's novels) just as the narrator
(also suffering a mania for perfection, also thwarted) torments
Wertheimer—

> I only visited Wertheimer in Traich to destroy him, to dis-
> turb and destroy him . . .

—forever bringing the conversation around to Glenn, reminding Wertheimer of Glenn, forcing the reluctant Wertheimer
to visit Glenn in New York (where Glenn calls him a loser
again). At the end, when Wertheimer needs him the most, the
narrator refuses to answer his letters.

> . . . my bad conscience, which was still troubled by the fact
> that I hadn't answered Wertheimer's letters, had more or
> less ignominiously abandoned him. . . .

Ultimately the narrator destroys Wertheimer by writing
about him. The narrator's version of Wertheimer is a loser; a
weak, indecisive, unoriginal cypher who tries to model himself
on, of all people, the narrator. "Weak characters never turn into
anything but weak artists," says the narrator, and "Wertheimer
confirms that theory absolutely."

The Loser, so well known for its irregularities, is a surprisingly
good example of the traditional novel devices of character
grouping and gradation and plot and subplot, albeit so forced
and exaggerated as to make them instances of what I call
stressed form; that is, the form is stressed to the point of
implausibility. The three principles—Gould, Wertheimer, and
the narrator—are all graded variations of the same character.
All three want to be piano virtuosos: Gould represents the limit,
the absolute artist whose ambition, skill and focus have carried him beyond the merely human piano artist; Wertheimer
and the narrator are similar versions of remarkable but merely
human accomplishment. They all have that lung disease, they're
all wealthy men, they all have country homes (Gould's is just
outside New York), they all stop playing the piano (Gould, of
course, famously stopped playing public concerts and retreated
to the recording studio). Wertheimer and the narrator are both
would-be suicides, they both end up writing books they cannot

finish and will ultimately destroy; Gould and Wertheimer die at almost the same moment, though for different reasons.

In other words their plot trajectories are parallel, almost identical in parts but with significant variation. In fact a good deal of Bernhard's comedy derives from his deadpan, obsessive forcing of the conventions of the well-made novel to the point of absurdity. He concentrates less on plot and psychological plausibility than on the extraordinary duplication and reduplication of situation, character and action (stressed form). His constant trope is hyperbole—and you know he is playing with technique as absurdity when he gives that lung disease, which is really his own lung disease, to the innkeeper as well (in this example, the narrator and the author momentarily are identical—another little game Bernhard plays with his reader).

> The innkeeper once had a lung disease like mine, I thought, like me she was able to squeeze this lung illness out of her, liquidate it with her will to live.

Wherein the Author Plays with Himself

This grid of receding narrators and repeating character traits and plot motifs supplies a matrix over which the author drapes his phantasmagoric riot of rhetorical substructures—repetition, antithesis, rant, digression, word play—all of which add drama, interest, and comedy to his text. It can't be emphasized enough how exuberant, ludic and, yes, obsessive Bernhard's style is.

One very common device, virtually a marker for Bernhardian prose, I call grammatical yoking. Grammatical yoking refers to grammatical structures meant to yoke two entities in a relationship of contrast or identity—e.g. just as, whereas, like/unlike, on the contrary, and some forms of subordination and psychological parallelism. In *The Loser*, there are multiple examples of each type mainly because much of the novel's text is concerned with establishing similarities and differences between the main characters. Bernhard never leaves a character alone in a sentence, is always contrasting, differentiating, refining. These yoking devices are a tool for elaboration (form creating content)—they seem to come automatically, even compulsively, to the author's pen—as well as a source of drama and conflict at the level of sentences.

[whereas] When it got cold, as Franz said, he would have his sister heat his room, **whereas** she wasn't allowed to heat her room.

[unlike] Wertheimer always set about his life with false assumptions, I said to myself, **unlike** Glenn who always set about his existence with the right assumptions.

[in contrast] She herself had never had enough money and never enough time and hadn't even been unhappy once, **in contrast** to those she called *refined gentlemen*, who always had enough money and enough time and constantly talked about their unhappiness.

[subordination by phrase] Wertheimer was the most passionate cemetery lover I have ever known, **even more passionate than me**, I thought.

[subordination by clause] Wertheimer hated Catholicism, **which his sister, as I also know, had completely fallen prey to in the last years.**

[parallelism] I never reproached myself for having money, I thought, **Wertheimer constantly reproached himself for it**, ...

It's important to recognize that Bernhard's texts are dense with this kind of rhetorical elaboration, that it is possible to analyze much of the text as a string or assemblage of such devices, such that a limited amount of plot material is made to vibrate and echo from sentence to sentence and page to page. Here is a short list of some of the other more spectacular devices Bernhard deploys. I give a minimal set of examples for each—you have to imagine the riot.

Parallel Construction:

So I go from one cage to the next, Wertheimer once said, from the Kohlmarkt apartment to Traich and then back again, he said, I thought. From the catastrophic big-city cage into the catastrophic forest cage. Now I hide myself here, now there, now in the Kohlmarkt perversity, now in the country-forest perversity.

[Here is an example of parallelism with variation by substitution.] Even the tiniest inn in Switzerland is clean and appetizing, even our finest Austrian hotels are filthy and unappetizing.

Paradox:

. . . I hated Glenn every moment, loved him at the same time with utmost consistency.

Fundamentally we are capable of everything, equally fundamentally we fail at everything . . .

Fugue Stop: This is my coinage for a special sort of retardation by repetition. The narrator suddenly seems trapped in a verbal loop, obsessively repeating the same thoughts and phrases, apparently unable to stop—and then, of course, finally he stops and continues with the narration.

> Wertheimer studied primarily in Vienna, not like me at the Mozarteum, but at the Vienna Academy, which the Mozarteum has always considered the better music conservatory, just as the Vienna Academy has always considered the Mozarteum the more useful school **[first instance].** Students always judge their own school to be something less than it is and cast an envious glance at their rival school **[second instance]**, above all music students are known for always giving much higher marks to their rival schools than their own, **[third instance]** and the Viennese music students always thought and believed the Mozarteum to be better, just as the Mozarteum students thought the Vienna Academy better **[fourth instance]**.

> Aphorism: "We get inside music completely or not at all. . . ." "Man is unhappiness . . ." ". . . desires are realized only when we are totally concentrated." ". . . we don't exist, we get existed, . . ." [And parodies of aphorisms] "If we stop drinking we die of thirst, if we stop eating we starve to death . . .".

Word spirals (repetition of a single word but something like a fugue stop):

> But everything we say is **nonsense**, he said, I thought, no matter what we say it is **nonsense** and our entire life is a single piece of **nonsense**. I understood that early on, I'd barely started to think for myself and I already understood that, we speak only **nonsense**, every thing we say is **nonsense**, but everything that is *said* to us is **nonsense**, like everything that is said at all, in this world only **nonsense**

has been said until now and, he said, only **nonsense** has actually and naturally been written, the writings we possess are only **nonsense** because they can only be **nonsense**, as history proves, he said, I thought.

Diatribe: At any moment, the narrator is apt to lapse into intemperate and hyperbolic invective against a pet target—partial list: Switzerland and the town of Chur, the Mozarteum, piano teachers, the countryside, Salzburg, Catholics, the Austrian judicial system, etc.

[on Switzerland and the mountain town of Chur, about a page long] . . . the Tyrolian mountains make me anxious. I've always hated the Vorarlberg, as I have Switzerland, where cretinism reigns supreme . . . the Churians struck me as despicable in their Alpine cretinism. . . . A person can be ruined for life in Chur, even if he spends only one night there.

The longest diatribe in the book belongs to Wertheimer (reported by the narrator), an attack on modern philosophy as nothing but bad aphorisms reduced from the books of the great philosophers of the past. It runs for six pages and, naturally, begins and ends with an aphorism.

Man is unhappiness, he said over and over, I thought, . . . [six pages later] death is the greatest misunderstanding of all, so Wertheimer, I thought.

Digression: These are distinct from diatribes which are a special instance of digression. Digression is a form of delay dramatized through suspension. In the following example, the innkeeper asks the narrator for a report on Wertheimer's

funeral upon which the narrator launches into a two-page discussion of real estate in Vienna and the Austrian economy—
note that the narrator identifies the passage as a digression for
the reader. Through the digression, the answer to the innkeeper's
request for details of Wertheimer's funeral is held in suspense,
and, naturally, as soon as the narrator returns to the subject of
the funeral he lapses into another digression. The ghost of Laurence Sterne haunts these pages; indeed, the narrator describes
his thoughts, that is, the entire text of the novel, as "these
Glenn- and Wertheimer-digressions."

> **. . . and so I sat down on the bed and gave a report.
> Naturally I could only give her a fragmentary report,**
> I started by saying I'd been to Vienna, occupied with the
> sale of my apartment, a large apartment I said . . . But I
> didn't sell the apartment . . . with the economic crisis we
> have today . . . [and so on for two pages, ending with]
> today's socialists are the new capitalists, all a sham, **I said
> to the innkeeper, who however didn't want to listen
> to my senseless digression, as I suddenly noticed, for
> she was still thirsting for my funeral report.**

Hyperbole: As I say, hyperbole underlies all Bernhard's
structural dispositions; it is the super-trope governing stressed
form. But sometimes Bernhard is just exuberantly hyperbolic
for the fun of it (or these could be described as mini-diatribes,
miniature lapses into intemperate invective).

> When it rains here for six or seven weeks without stop-
> ping and the local inhabitants go crazy in this unstoppable
> rain, I thought, one has to have tremendous discipline not
> to kill oneself. **But half the people here kill themselves
> sooner or later. . . .**

What lousy teachers we had to put up with, teachers who screwed up our heads. **Art destroyers all of them, art liquidators, culture assassins, murderers of students.**

Allegorical Set-piece: The authorial lung disease shared by four characters in the novel is a good example of the way Bernhard is always interacting playfully with the real world through the text. It is his personal and factual lung disease growing microbial on the page. But Bernhard also uses allegorical set-pieces to connect *The Loser* with (to create a dramatic implied conversation with—this is its aesthetic function, to create textual interest by multiplying dramatic exchanges) a larger historical context, especially Austria's history with Nazis and the Holocaust. Naturally Wertheimer is Jewish and likes to visit his family crypt where a clearly allegorical beech tree "growing out of the crypt had progressively dislodged the immense granite block inscribed with the names of all the Wertheimers." An extended (three pages) example of allegorical set-piece occurs when the three young piano students rent a house together outside of Salzburg, "the house of a recently deceased Nazi sculptor . . . who had worked for years in the service of Hitler." The rooms are crowded with monstrous marble "eyesores", too large to be removed but which, ironically, improve the acoustics.

Ironic Mis-appropriation of Fact: Bernhard's fictional dramatic confrontation with reality goes beyond the comic use of his own lung disease and allegorical reference to the use of an actual person Glenn Gould in his text, which is actually a misuse for he gets Glenn Gould glaringly and hilariously wrong on purpose.

Glenn Gould was a real life Canadian piano virtuoso who earned instant fame for his early recording of Bach's *Goldberg Variations*. And he did stop performing publicly at the height of his celebrity after a brief career. Beyond that he bears no resemblance to Glenn Gould in Bernhard's novel. Gould never studied with Horowitz (Horowitz never taught), never studied in Salzburg, didn't speak German fluently, never had a country place outside of New York (he lived most of his life in Toronto), his parents weren't wealthy, and he died of a stroke at 50, not 51, in his sleep, not at the piano playing the *Goldberg Variations*. The real Glenn Gould was a prolific author of essays and scripts unlike the fictional Glenn Gould who, the narrator claims, didn't write at all. These are deliberate distortions of fact in order to create a Glenn Gould who conforms to the needs of the novel's structure and also to juice the novel's dramatic encounter with reality, the real world beyond the text. Bernhard's bold-faced, flat-out lies about Glenn Gould are immensely comic in part because it is so obvious that he is playing that game: What is true here? What is false? And what is a half-truth based upon a truth?

In the novel Gould is portrayed as the ideal of the romantic artist, a genius, eccentric, self-conscious, obsessive, concentrated, and immune to the doubt that plagues his friends. But he is also arrogant, cruel and inhuman.

> Glenn Gould *said the word loser out loud in a crucial moment*, I thought. We say a word and destroy a person.

His is the gnomic wisdom of high art.

> We get inside music completely or not at all, Glenn often said . . .

But he is also an exuberant dimwit who runs outside his rented house and impetuously chops down a tree, a half-metre thick, that "obstructed his playing" before it occurs to him that he could just pull the blinds. (He also gets drunk and pops champagne corks at the Nazi statues.)

Glenn Gould thus is another paradox in a novel built on contradictions: he's a joke rendered from real life with precisely erroneous detail, a buffoonish version of the Nietzschean overman as a piano-playing Paul Bunyan; but he is also the image of the transcendent artist, the pure artist, who spends his life perfecting himself as an instrument. None of this is real or meant to be real.

Irony, or the Double Sign of Difficulty

Except for the first page, as I say, the entire novel consists of one paragraph of character thought, a single, unstoppable column of prose weaving in and out of content topics, plot and figure and trope, without a discrete stop along the way (Bernhard will even shift from one content stream to another on a comma in the middle of a sentence, with no logical or grammatical transition), so that it is all a trope, an image, oddly fragmented but with the fragments glued back together such that it resembles the thought-ravings of a madman who cannot control the logorrheic flow, not even minimally by breaking it into conventional logical segments called paragraphs.

Over and over, the reader senses that the narrator is thinking fast to prevent himself from thinking, his thoughts always implying an excess they dare not express (although the narrator does let slip many very clear pointers). The entire text is framed within an implied conflict—the narrator's resistance to a truth he cannot face—and this conflict propels the text forward with a mysterious urgency. The desperate, compulsive, and transparently self-serving if not delusional nature of the narrator's thoughts in turn motivates the stressed form characteristic of the prose. Hysteria motivates hyperbole. The mechanical elaborations of grammatical yoking are desperate attempts on the part of the narrator to appear logical and analytical even as he is constantly dropping into spiraling word repetitions, fugue stops, digressions, and self-revealing tirades.

But the disorder is only a semblance of disorder. It looks like a verbal torrent, the delirium of a madman, which of course it is meant to resemble in some superficial and theatrical sense, a deranged dramatic monologue (of thought), when in fact it is also artfully controlled, patterned and symmetrical (right down to the substandard Ehrbar piano the narrator plays as a child which *returns* at the end of the novel as the rented, "horribly untuned" Ehrbar Wertheimer plays for his travesty concert), art as symptom or symptom as art (repetition is a pattern of art and also of dream and neurosis), super-controlled (such an Austrian trait) and at the same time in tension with its own apparent haphazardness and compulsivity.

Hyperbole and absurdity subvert every aspect of Bernhard's novel; hyperbole is the constant marker for irony, the double sign that destroys the fictional facade of plausibility and univocal meaning and points to a second meaning that is absent in the text. This is the ultimate moment of ambiguity and difficulty, the text announcing that it doesn't mean what it says it means.

There are reasons for this difficulty, this incomprehensibility. One reason (perhaps the least interesting) is political, the collapse of trust in the German language shared by almost all thinking writers of German after the Second World War. This is perhaps true in spades for Austrian writers, coming from a country whose unforced complicity in that Nazi horror show is still denied. How do you write the truth in a language of lies (when the Nazi statues are so huge they can't be moved out of the cultural house)? The answer is that you draw attention to the corruption of the German language by writing in corrupt, unbeautiful, incorrect, unclear German. You use language to attack itself. If language cannot express the truth, the secret horror at the back of history, then you write in a way that draws attention to the paradox of writing in a language that cannot write the truth—in so doing, you somehow draw attention to, implicate, limn, the truth.

A second reason for incomprehensibility is philosophical. Kant drew a line between the real world and the world of existence (where we live): absolutes, God, the Good, Beauty and Truth on one side of the line; science, but also fallible humans, uncertainty, ambiguity, and doubt on the other. All so-called knowledge is limited to the phenomenal or existential world, all knowledge is human; that is, as Kant wrote, "It must be possible for the 'I think' to accompany all my representations"—*The Loser* reads as if Bernhard assimilated this sentence and made it his stylistic talisman. But paradoxically even the conscious subject, the person who thinks, cannot appear to itself as an object; the heart cannot know its reasons.

The great Viennese (wealthy, Jewish, neurasthenic, suicidal) philosopher Ludwig Wittgenstein drew the noose even tighter by defining language as a limiting concept; ultimately language cannot speak the truth but can only talk about itself, *play* with itself (pun intended). Modern philosophy after Kant is famously *difficult* stylistically, mainly because philosophers have had to work around the central problem that, *by definition*, they cannot talk about what they are talking about.

Difficulty and *incomprehensibility* become aesthetic virtues after Kant (perhaps not what he intended); clarity and formal neatness are marks of fantasy or prevarication. Hence the tradition of German Romanticism, a paradoxical aesthetic based on the impossibility of creating beauty. What goes for beauty (in novels, paintings, symphonies) are only failed attempts to create beauty, which is otherworldly, unconditioned, absolute, sublime (in the Kantian sense) and beyond language. German Romanticism is a *hyper-realist* aesthetic in the sense that it values works of art that represent their own inevitable *failure*. In contrast to the ideal of classical unity, it values fragments, digressions, interruptions, mixed forms, incompleteness, *difficulty*, and, above all, irony.

Friedrich Schlegel famously defended *difficulty* in his essay "On Incomprehensibility," which is really an essay about the role of irony in a post-Kantian literature. Irony in its original form comes in two basic varieties: 1) Socratic irony which is the cunning use of dissimulation to make a point; and 2) the ancient Greek dramatic device of *parabasis*, the moment when the chorus turns away from the other actors and addresses the audience directly. Irony is that moment in a text when the author glances up at the reader and says, You realize, of course, that this isn't real, that what I put on the page is not what I mean. (Always the literalist, Plato condemned Ironists at the same time as Sophists and Poets.) To German Romantics, the novel is the great modern example of ironic form, and the novel tradition out of which they write begins with Cervantes' *Don Quixote* (a book about an insane person, about 50, in a quest for the absolute) and descends through Laurence Sterne and Denis Diderot, the masters of digression, delay and self-parody.

"A Scrupulous Fidelity"

About his own ironic style Jacques Derrida once wrote, "I have this attitude that some people must have perceived as double, of emancipation, revolt, irony, and at the same time a scrupulous fidelity." It is to this aspect of "scrupulous fidelity" we must now attend.

The Loser is very much a *novel-as-performance*, both image and allegory, more image than discursive thought yet very much a novel of ideas with the ideas implicit in the structure, action, and style. Besides the aesthetics of German Romanticism *The Loser* reflects a conception of art inherited from Schopenhauer—especially Schopenhauer's notion that art itself is the intermediary between the supra-sensory and the merely human, that in creating or correctly appreciating great art we enter an eternal realm of Platonic Ideas (Beauty, God, or even Being in Heidegger's sense) and leave the tawdry realm of existence behind (what Bernhard's narrator calls "the existence machine").

The Loser fictionalizes the European version of nostalgia for Being (the American version is a retreat to fundamentalist Christianity) and a sense of living in a fallen existential world. It presents three men whose goal is to become transcendent artists; one succeeds, the other two fail, and their psychomachia is rather a soul-unmaking or disintegration leading to paralysis and the one authentic act left, suicide. Glenn Gould is the virtuoso, the genius, the perfect instrument. Albeit, he is also unconsciously cruel and a buffoon. But there are passages in *The Loser* where the irony seems to lift and some deeper reality is revealed.

> The second he [Gould] sat down at the piano he sank into himself, I thought, he looked like an animal then, on closer inspection like a cripple, on even closer inspection like the sharp-witted, beautiful man that he was.

Gould is only perfect, only beautiful (and nothing else in the novel is described as "beautiful") when he is playing. This is the hierophantic moment, the ur-moment to which Bernhard returns throughout the novel, starting with the scene in Salzburg, when the narrator and Wertheimer overhear Gould playing the *Goldberg Variations* and are destroyed, and repeating (insisting) through to the novel's close, the *Goldberg Variations* on the record player, the narrator alone in Wertheimer's empty bedroom at Traich.

The way Bernhard distorts the facts of Gould's death makes thematic sense, having him die of a stroke at "the perfect moment", that is, while playing the *Goldberg Variations* instead of, as was in fact the case, during his sleep. Gould achieves transcendence through his art, he goes "beyond the limit" and attains "the inhuman state"; the narrator and Wertheimer meanwhile fail, dazzled, paralyzed, crippled by fear, and caught in what the narrator calls the existential trap. *The Loser* is all aftermath, a narrative of disintegration, laced with transparent self-hatred, denial, and resentment, obsessively circling back on itself, always returning to the ur-moment, the fatal confrontation with genius. Having attempted to reach the heights, they fall back into the crippled world of the merely human, Kant's phenomenal world, imperfect, ambiguous, clouded.

> We look at people and see only cripples, Glenn once said to us, physical or mental or mental *and* physical, there are no others, I thought. The longer we look at someone the more crippled he appears to us. . . . The word is full of cripples.

Every great novel possesses a mysterious flickering quality, the on/off light of irony, that conceals and reveals its moment of fidelity. *The Loser* presents the image of the fallen world (Kierkegaard's "present age") haunted by the idea of goodness, tormented by beauty, a losers' world, a metaphoric Land of the Dead where only conditional motives and mediated relationships are possible, ruled by language and the Imaginary, where people are trapped in a relation of reflexive creation. Like Hegel's master and slave the narrator and Wertheimer (Wertheimer and his sister) need each other in order to exist, and that relation can easily be reduced to the negative: I need to crush him in order to exist just as he needs to crush me in order to exist.

But the image of a fallen world implies its opposite; this is the mimetic paradox. Bernhard riddles out the unseen world of the Absolute, of Beauty and the Good, in the narrator's contorted prose. The style is a vehicle for meaning, the prose con-torted because it is reaching beyond the limit of language. In the end, we can only imagine through art what it might be like to have perfect clarity of action and thought, to be Glenn Gould.

PEDRO, THE UNCANNY

A NOTE ON JUAN RULFO'S
PEDRO PÁRAMO

JOURNEYS to the Land of the Dead usually fall under the rubric of the epic. We think of Odysseus talking with the shades of ancient heroes while they drink blood to help remember what it was like to be warm and alive, or Dante touring the punishments of Hell, or Orpheus chasing Eurydice into the Underworld. The ancients peopled the afterlife with, well, people, imagining it as a rather large and dreary retirement community.

Juan Rulfo is Mexican and as such has a foot in the ancient world of myth and epic. In writing *Pedro Páramo*, he is often credited with inventing Latin American Magic Realism and the novel of the *cacique*, the thuggish, semi-feudal autocrats of post-colonial New Spain. It's tempting to draw a line from the *Inferno* to *Pedro Páramo* and from *Pedro Páramo* to *Autumn of the Patriarch*. Rulfo's vision is Meso-American tinged with Medieval Catholicism. His novel is local, folkloric, and paradoxically modern—dissociated, fragmented, and unemotional.

His characters are peasants, priests, cowboys and village women, but their fractured stories seem voiced in the mannered, modernist fashion of Samuel Beckett's plays. Rulfo's novelistic vision of death is Dante-esque, grim, grotty—endless consciousness in a cramped, damp grave.

Pedro Páramo is 125 pages long and split into 57 unnumbered subsections or fragments that range in length from a few lines to several pages. It starts out in the first person in the voice of Juan Preciado, Pedro Páramo's son by an estranged and abandoned wife, but then develops several narrative lines and points of view. There are multiple third person point of view sections (Pedro Páramo, a priest named Father Renteria, Páramo's wife, and various villagers) and a few italicized sections which are mostly Pedro Páramo's thoughts about his childhood love, a girl named Susana (who later marries him, goes insane and dies). About halfway through the book, Juan Preciado's first person narration turns into a dialogue between Juan and a village woman named Dorotea who, apparently, was buried in the same grave with him.

Like the similarly fractured chronology, the fractured point of view structure is motivated within the text by the fact that the characters are all dead. They speak as ghostly "voices" or as people who look real enough but are, in fact, moribund. Released from their bodies, no longer tethered to place or time, these spirit memories seem to float in and out of the text, not to mention triggering the occasional personal identity crises.

> I could hear the dogs barking, as if I had wakened them. I saw a man cross the street.
> "You!" I called.
> "You!" he called back. In my own voice.

The point is that when you are dead you no longer have to follow the rules of logic: you are no longer anywhere, you are no longer anchored to a particular time and you may no longer be yourself.

Pedro Páramo starts with Juan Preciado deciding to return to the village of Comala after his mother's death because she wanted him to go back and find his father Pedro Páramo and "Make him pay for the way he forgot us." A couple of pages later Juan meets a burro driver named Abundio who claims also to be Páramo's son and tells him their father is dead. Juan reaches Comala, which, as everyone he meets agrees, looks dead. And the villagers he encounters demonstrate preternatural qualities to an alarming degree. They vanish, or talk to the dead (several seem to have a direct line to his deceased mother), or hear and see events to which Juan himself is not privy.

Growing alarmed and depressed, Juan seeks refuge with a couple who are in bed naked together and turn out to be brother and sister. He sleeps with the sister, the room they inhabit becomes more and more tomb-like, and finally Juan undergoes some sort of crisis which may or may not be his own death or the realization that he is dead. For the rest of the novel, when he appears, he is in the grave talking to Dorotea and listening to voices from other graves.

Between the snippets Juan overhears in the cemetery and the fragmentary third-person point of view scenes which make up the bulk of the text, the reader manages to piece together the story of what has happened in Comala, the epic tale of the rise and fall of the eponymous Pedro Páramo, murderous hacien-dado, wealthy landowner, corrupt and predatory. Páramo's story begins with scenes from his childhood, his landowner father's murder, the moment when the young Pedro takes over the reins of his father's flagging empire (like Michael Corleone in *The Godfather*), the rise of his fortunes through a cynical mar-riage (to Juan Preciado's mother), murder, coercion, bribery and political manipulations.

Ruthless, sociopathic Páramo lacks for only one thing, his childhood friend Susana. Thirty years after she left Comala, she returns with her father (another incestuous something-or-other seems implied). Páramo arranges the father's murder, marries Susana and then watches her slip into insanity and death. Shortly after he buries her, he is knifed to death by one of his own illegitimate offspring, the burro driver Abundio from the novel's opening (at the opening, he is already dead but still walking around and talking).

This event, unlike the rest of the novel, is datable from internal evidence—Dorotea tells Juan (in their grave) that "not long before he died the Cristero's revolted"; the Cristero Rebellion lasted from 1926 to 1929 and the diplomatic rapprochement at the end of that conflict ushered in the political system that has governed Mexico ever since. Though *Pedro Páramo* is about death, and all its characters are ghosts, the novel is less interested in the fact of death and its relationship to self, less metaphysical, as it were, than it is in the existential relationship of heirarchy and control in historical Mexico.

In telling Pedro Páramo's story—and this is key to the novel's amazing reputation—Rulfo is also telling the story of modern Mexico. Pedro Páramo is a metonym for the semi-feudal land-owning class which has bedeviled Mexican politics and development from colonial times. Adept at supporting the winning side, even when the winning side set out to redistribute the land and end the haciendado system, men like Páramo managed to turn the great peasant rebellions of 1910 to 1920 to their advantage, crushing the peasants and sucking the lifeblood out of rural Mexico. The novel is then a metaphor for Mexican history.

But *Pedro Páramo* is also a love story, albeit a love story nailed to the grid of power relations; Pedro Páramo's lifelong desire for Susana animates the final sequence of actions in his story, which is good because after walking to town and finding himself in a graveyard Juan Preciado, himself, fails to accomplish much.

(*Pedro Páramo* also contains a third strong plot—amidst a range of lesser plots—which involves the priest Father Renteria whose moral struggle with his own acquiescence to Pedro Páramo's corruption is one of the more fascinating and dramatic elements of the book.)

The dead are everywhere in Mexico just as they are in Rulfo's novel. I googled the Cristero Rebellion out of curiosity and found archives of photographs of firing squad executions, lopped heads, telephone poles marching into the distance, bodies dangling from the cross-bars. In Mexico they have the Day of the Dead and waxy, skeletal, dead Christs in the sanctuaries of their churches, and the daily newspapers parade the daily dead in contorted, bloody splendour on their front pages. Drug cartels have replaced the warlords and *caciques*, Pedro Páramo *redivivus*, not a single man but a resilient and self-re-inventing social structure that dates back to Cortez and his ruthless captains ("ruthless" is of course a feeble epithet, their taste for gold and blood was revolting and uncanny).

On a certain level (when speaking of great novels it is always necessary to specify levels), *Pedro Páramo* is utterly realistic, its fractured structure merely reflecting a culture in which life is always being interrupted by death, where the originary personal consciousness is constantly canceled by the bullet (where poor souls are sealed in drums of acid or buried in mass graves to erase their memories). *Pedro Páramo* is an historical novel written out of a country absent a strong central government, without a core of structural continuity, where a kind of demonic violence trumps the personal and the national, a country continually restarting itself and betraying itself.

Only an anti-novel could emerge from such spiritual miasma. There is no history and no novel, just the endless retrospective present of the grave and a structure that reflects Viktor Shklovsky's idea of aesthetic strangeness (content contorted in the artificial symmetries of form) and Freud's concept of the uncanny (the dread-haunted familiar). The form of *Pedro Páramo* is stressed or forced, unconventional in the modernist mode, but not modernist in inspiration, as I say, completely original and realistic *on a certain level*, that is from the point of view of the dead (and Mexican culture), and uncanny in the sense that characters *seem* alive when they are not, they walk and talk and even make love but are dead.

The structure of death, the thematic forcing of diction and repetition, is evident from the beginning. On the first short page of *Pedro Páramo*, we have "dying," "died" and "dead." Moving forward, the town of Comala looks "dead", it's deserted, the air is "dead" and Juan Preciado describes it as a "dead village." Juan's mother is dead on the first page, his father Pedro Páramo is dead, it turns out that Abundio, the burro driver he talked to on his way to the village, is dead. A woman disappears then suddenly appears and crosses the street in front of him, he hears voices. "Especially voices. And here where the air was so dead, they sounded even louder."

The word "dream" also recurs, as do "voices" and "murmurs"—apparently Rulfo thought, for a while, of calling the novel *Murmurs*. "It was the voices that killed me," Juan says, when he finally realizes he's dead. "The voices killed me."

> And those murmurs seemed to come from the walls, to seep out of the cracks and broken spots. They were the peoples' voices but they weren't clear, they were almost secret, as if they were whispering something to me as I passed. . . .

All of Rulfo's characters react with deadpan (sorry) acceptance, passive in the face of their own morbidity. The effect is uncanny, zombie-like, they are the living dead, strange mirror images of the living. But an immediate consequence of relentless repetition, verbal and structural, is the creation of a fictionally plausible Land of the Dead, a graveyard *faux* epic composed of whispers and gossip.

Note how skillfully Rulfo leads the reader by degrees into a metaphysical complacency. At the start of *Pedro Páramo*, Juan Preciado, like the reader, depends for an explanation of the premises of the new world of the novel on the characters he meets along the way. (This is true of all novels but particularly so in a novel that outs its fictional nature from the first words.) From a distance the town looks dead and deserted; Abundio, the burro driver, tells him, "That isn't how it looks. It is. Nobody lives there anymore." This a pun. There are people in the town, but they are dead.

The first person Juan sees in the village disappears "as if she didn't even exist." Trying to find a room for the night, he hunts up a woman named Dona Eduviges who seems to be expecting him. It turns out she is somehow in touch with Juan's mother. When he tells her his mother is dead, Dona Eduviges' only reaction is to say, ". . . then that's why her voice sounded so weak."

A few pages later, he tells her about meeting Abundio and his burros on the way to the village. Dona Eduviges says, ". . . Abundio's dead. I'm sure he must be dead. Didn't he tell you?" Death is reduced to the level of an everyday fact in the tone of her words. Juan Preciado observes: "I thought the woman must be crazy. Then I didn't think anything at all, except that I must be in some other world. My body seemed to be floating . . .". At which point, the reader thinks: Uh-oh! Other world, other rules.

And a few pages after that, Juan, beginning to know the new world, asks a woman who has befriended him, "Are you alive, Damiana? Tell me, Damiana?" Suddenly, she vanishes. And still a few more pages along, given shelter by a couple, he asks outright, "Are you dead?" At this point, he has learned to ask the right questions. Soon he realizes he's dead himself and a few pages after that Damiana explains how she was buried in his grave with his arms around her and how the voices he hears come from nearby graves. Thus, by easy but clearly defined steps or stages, Rulfo has told us we're in another world (Land of the Dead) and the basic mechanisms of that world.

Rulfo packs his little novel with action, but every plot leads to death or through death. The images of death are shatteringly present and macabre but strangely hollowed out; they produce horror and anxiety (the uncanny) without emotional release. First, of course, there is the necessary death scene of the dead hero, or at least Juan Preciado's realization (*anagnorisis*) of his own death, a moment that is figurative and dream-like, an absolutely uncanny reversal (*peripeteia*) in which the zombie realizes it's a zombie—and the reader feels like a sweater turning itself inside out.

The moment arrives in two discrete segments, the one subjective (Juan) and the other an objective report (Dorotea). This is how Juan Preciado experiences his death:

> . . . I got up, but the woman went on sleeping. Her mouth was open and a bubbling sound came out of it, like the death-rattle.
>
> I went out into the street for a little air, but the heat followed me out and wouldn't go away. There wasn't any air. Only the silent, stupefied night, scorched by the August dog days.
>
> There wasn't any air. I had to swallow the same air I breathed out, holding it back with my hands so it wouldn't

escape. I could feel it coming and going, and each time it was less and less, until it got so thin it slipped through my fingers forever.

Forever.

I remember seeing something like a cloud of foam, and washing myself in the foam, and losing myself in the cloud. That was the last thing I saw.

And this is Dorotea's report of the same event.

". . . I found you in the plaza, a long way from Donis's house, and he was right there with me, telling me you were dying. We dragged you into the shadow of the arcade, and you were having convulsions, the way people die of fright. If there wasn't any air on the night you talk about, how did we have the strength to bring you out here and bury you? And you can see that we buried you."

The two versions conflict. Juan Preciado thinks he died of suffocation. Dorotea thinks he died of fright. Subsequently, Juan agrees that it was the voices that killed him, the voices of the dead. The effect is to evoke denial and assimilation by degrees—the *anagnorisis* itself mimes the slow-motion consciousness of the living dead.

Rulfo is especially good at metonymic detail. Rather than supply the reader with full-on clinical realism, Rulfo implicates the act of dying in a series of carefully selected images (thus saving himself a lot of space—the novel is written like a telegram). Locked in a bare bedroom the first night by Dona Eduviges, Juan Preciado hears someone shout, "The hell with life anyway!" and then again, "Let me kick! You can hang me, but let me kick!" And then we learn that this is where Páramo's henchman

hanged the farmer Toribio Aldrete and the death screams con-
jure the horrid images of the hanging body and its spasmodic
death throes.

Dona Eduviges' death sneaks up on the reader, replicating
Juan Preciado's own staggered realizations and the uncanny
quality of the book as a whole. An early description has her "so
pale, you would think there wasn't any blood in her body." A
little later we find out she committed suicide. "That's how she
died, with the blood choking her. I can still see her expressions.
They were the most pitiful expressions a human being ever
made."

Juan Preciado's friend-lover-grave partner Dorotea dies by
simply giving up. "I opened my mouth so it [her soul] could
leave, and it left. I felt something fall into my hands. It was a little thread of blood that had tied it to my heart." Juan Preciado's
mother dies of sorrow. Don Fulgor Sedano, Páramo's fat fore-
man, is slaughtered by rebels, forced to run while they shoot
him down "with one foot on the ground and one foot in the
air."

Some of the deaths are elided. We never see Pedro
Páramo's son Miguel die, tossed from his horse going over a
jump. But Dona Eduviges hears the horse's hooves on the road
(over and over, as I say, Rulfo seeks to pin a specific concrete
metonymic image to a death) and when Miguel comes to the
door, confused because he can't find the village he was riding
towards, she tells him, "You're not crazy, Miguel. You're dead."

Pedro Páramo orders Susana's father Don Bartolome mur-
dered at a mine far from town. We never see the murder, but
some ghostly presence appears to Susana that night (and she
dreams or seems to dream about a cat that gets into her room
and curls up between her legs, some eerie sexual reference).

"Your father's dead, Susana. He died the night before last,
and they came here today to tell us they've already buried

him. They couldn't bring him here because it's too far. You're all alone now, Susana."

"So it *was* my father." She smiled. "He came here to say good-bye to me," she said, and smiled.

One image of death that is not physical but moral develops out of the Catholicism represented by the character named Father Renteria. Called to Susana's bedside to get her to repent and receive communion, the priest is taken for her dead lover Florencio. Renteria cruelly sows her addled brain with horrific death images to persuade her to take the sacrament, forcing her to repeat his words, his macabre litany of death.

> "I swallow the froth of my saliva. I eat clods of earth. They are crawling with worms. They choke my throat and rasp against my palate . . . My lips loosen, grimacing, and my teeth rend and devour them. My face dissolves, my eyes melt to slime, my hair goes up in flames . . .".

This lovely man is actually, so far as I can tell, the only one in the book to get out alive. He runs off to the mountains to join the revolution, probably the Cristero movement mentioned above. But before that he pronounces himself dead, spiritually dead. "I died. I'm the corpse."

Rulfo distributes the structures of time distortion throughout his novel, as I have said, forcing the thematics of death conceptually onto the fragmented narrative. He uses abrupt narrative breaks and leaps to distort the reader's experience of time. Meanwhile he avoids most conventional time-switch devices, the sort of bread-and-butter narrative guides that tell the reader when events occur relative to other events.

For example, right at the beginning of the novel he uses a distinctive shadowing technique in which he gives scene and scene set-up in reversed order. On the second page, we find this fragment of dialogue inserted without preamble or context. Rulfo doesn't even give the usual dialogue attributions to let the reader know who is talking.

"What's the name of that village down there?"
"Comala, senor."
"You're sure it's Comala?"
"Yes, senor."
"Why does it look so dead?"

This dialogue is between Juan Preciado and Abundio, the burro driver, although the reader doesn't figure this out until later. The scene continues for about a page at which point Juan mentions that his father is Pedro Páramo. His companion (Abundio) gasps and then, abruptly, we get the introduction to the scene oddly inserted at the climactic moment of the scene itself (my italics for clarity).

But the way he said it, it was almost like a gasp. I said, "At least that's what they told me his name was."
I heard him say, "Oh," again.
I met him in Los Encuentros, where three or four roads come together. I was just waiting there, and finally he came by with his burros.
"Where are you going?" I asked him.
"That way, senor," he said, pointing.
"Do you know where Comala is?"
"That's where I'm going."
So I followed him. I walked along behind, keeping up with his steps, until he understood I was following him and slowed down a little. After that we walked side by side, almost touching shoulders.
He said, "Pedro Páramo is my father too."

Note how Rulfo, when he inserts the set-back in time, deliberately avoids the grammatically correct tense change. "I *had* met him in Los Encuentro . . .". Note also how he elides any transition back into the scene in progress. It's as if he simply lifted the beginning of the sequence with Abundio and stuck it in somewhere else to create this dreamy, disjointed effect. Lest the reader think he made a mistake, Rulfo nails his authorial intention by repeating the technique a couple of pages later— another instance of thematic encoding or forcing at the structural level.

Rulfo also employs a kind of narrative syncopation: he mentions or alludes to an incident without expanding on it, then fills in the whole scene later in the text. For example, Dorotea mentions to Juan Preciado that Father Renteria told her she would never get to Heaven for her sins; fourteen pages later Rulfo gives us the full scene—Dorotea coming to confession and Renteria's cruel refusal. On another occasion, Dorotea tells Juan how, after Susana's death, Pedro Páramo "spent the rest of his life hunched over in a chair, looking at the road where they took her out to bury her." Then 38 pages later we are given the more or less continuous narrative of Susana's death, Páramo's grief and his murder in the chair by the side of the road.

And sometimes Rulfo uses a rather lovely temporal weaving. Near the middle of the novel there is a sequence that begins with a group of local Indians coming to Comala to market their goods, staying most of the day, then packing and leaving in the rain.

> The Indians packed up their wares at dusk, and stepped out into the rain with their heavy bundles on their shoulders. They went into the church to pray to the Virgin, and left her a bunch of thyme as an offering. Then they set out for Apango.

Without a line break, the narrative shifts to a scene between Susana and her nurse-caretaker Justina.

> Justina Diaz went into Susana San Juan's bedroom and put a bunch of rosemary on the wall bracket.

(Note the elegant *anadiplosis*—"bunch of thyme" "bunch of rosemary"—which links the two distinct passages.)

What follows is a strange, eerie scene, a mix of ghosts and madness, heralding the murder of Susana's father far away. There's a scream, he seems to appear as a ghost and tries to send Justina away, a cat sleeps between Susana's legs (a delicate sexual innuendo, unsettling, bizarre). After a line break, Rulfo inserts a mysterious flashback scene in which Susana's father lowers her into an abandoned mineshaft into a heap of human bones. Flickering in and out, the rain repeats.

> The rain was turning to hail, muffling all sounds except its own.

> The rain pattered on the banana leaves. It sounded as if the raindrops were boiling in the water that stood on the earth.
> The sheets were cold and damp. The drains gushed and foamed, working all day, all night, all day. The water ran and ran, hissing with a million bubbles.

And again at the close of the sequence.

> It was still raining. The Indians had gone. It was Monday, and the Comala valley was still drowned in rain.

In *Pedro Páramo* the way to the Land of the Dead is through a fissure (like Dante's cave) in the text—"the gap I had come through," recalls Juan Preciado, "like an open wound in the blackness of the mountains." I am reminded of the opening of Thomas Mann's "Death in Venice"—Aschenbach walking to the North Cemetery, "the neighborhood quite empty" and the stonemason's yard opposite creating "a supernumerary and untenanted graveyard opposite the real one" and the mortuary chapel with its portico and staircase guarded by "two apocalyptic beasts" and the motto "They are entering into the House of the Lord." Equally, I am reminded of the opening of Conrad's "Heart of Darkness" and a similar entryway into the phantasmal universe: Marlow travels to Brussels to secure an appointment, the Company offices are situated in a house "as still as a house in the city of the dead." He walks through an outer room past two enigmatic women knitting (Norns, Fates), "guarding the door of Darkness, knitting black wool as for a pall."

I cite these parallels in part to show that Rulfo is fairly in line with traditional literary motifs, that there is a kind of conventionality to his unconventionality (not to diminish his originality, but to recognize the existence of traditions within traditions). It is a convention that heroes go off the path, squeeze through gates, pass through magic doors, fall asleep, or travel to the Land of the Dead—anything to get them metaphorically out of the ordinary and into a place of meaning (secrets, Being, the Unconscious, the ineffable and unknowable). Getting beyond (whatever *beyond* is), motivates insight (*anagnorisis*) but it also motivates formal variation (intensity, riot, verbal play).

In the ancient epics, the Land of the Dead really was the home of the shades whereas modern writers tend to make it a metaphor, an allegory, or a device of rhetorical context. Rulfo's fantastic structural and technical pyrotechnics are doubly or triply motivated. First, there is a political and cultural focus—Mexico's obsession with the dead, its horrific past, its failure to create a political identity against the centrifugal forces of demonic violence. No ordinary language can paint this picture; conventional structure would force a conventional narrative arc and a false totality on what remains a dark mystery.

Form reflects ideology. There is a common sense way of speaking that eventuates, more or less, in the conventional realistic novel, which is (really) just as formally committed as a modernist experiment but pretends to a comforting verisimilitude that amounts to a spiritual complacency. I am who I think I am, the world is intelligible, my adventures have a predictable arc of development. Another sort of novel reflects a more complicated vision of existence and a different history (or version of history). Just as in German-speaking countries where the language itself became suspect after the atrocities of the Second World War, Mexican authors like Rulfo attempt to incorporate in the language of their texts their country's horrendous history of genocide and constant revolution. In *Pedro Páramo* the dead have a voice; in fact, only the dead get to speak; every word is uttered in the Land of the Dead.

To go one step further, a novel like *Pedro Páramo* subverts the entire Enlightenment project, the belief in an autonomous thinking subject, in reason, and in human progress (perhaps America is now the only country in the world that still pays lip service to that bit of 18th century flim-flam). By projecting an uncanny, cracked mirror image of the quotidian onto the pages of his book, Rulfo lets loose the demons and ghosts that haunt all our histories. He escapes the anaesthetic *faux* humanism of contemporary market-driven fiction and establishes his work of art as something close to an eruption of the thing we cannot talk about but which insists on its presence nonetheless. He brings it close, close enough to touch, and the novel smells of the fresh-dug soil of the grave.

BEFORE/AFTER
HISTORY
AND THE NOVEL

Novels and History, an Exercise in Dialectics

HE DIFFERENCE between written history and novels is contained in the difference between two theories of truth: truth in history is denotative or evidentiary while truth in novels is defined by coherence. It's as simple as that. Yet they both rise from the same internal source in the mind, the story-making source, the imagination. This makes history and novels, at some level, teasingly similar. And then, of course, we do use that word "truth" in discussing novels in a loose and sloppy way that leads to all sorts of confusion. When we ask if a novel seems true, we often mean whether it sounds authentic, whether it's plausible, whether the characters could have existed or events transpired. Sometimes "truth" in this context refers to emotional truth, an even more subjective truth than verisimilitude. As a novelist I have often found that what seems perfectly plausible to me in an emotional vein can be incredible to other people (readers).

But the fact remains that when you want to test the truth of an historical assertion you have recourse ultimately to documentary or archaeological evidence, whereas when you want to test the truth of a novelistic assertion you can only look at the text. It makes no sense to ask what Sancho Panza said or looked like outside *Don Quixote*, whereas you can test the claim that George Washington had false teeth or Sir John A. Macdonald occasionally drank too much by examining documents from the period. This is the reason for a secondary difference between history and novels: historical explanations change when new evidence surfaces, whereas no fact in the world at large can force an author to rewrite a novel.

This is not to deny, of course, that there are sometimes criticisms of novels in terms of plausibility or truth, especially when it comes to historical novels. When you write an historical novel, you accept a certain contractual relationship with the reader in terms of verisimilitude, that quality of seeming to be real, which is one of the signal attributes of realistic fiction. But in fiction this contract can be fairly loose. When I wrote my novel *Elle*, it made sense to get the dates right and the proper sequence of events, not to mention the correct king in France at the time. Readers accustomed to verisimilitude in novels are easily distracted by obvious mistakes of so-called historical fact. But a reader's knowledge of any particular era is usually shallow, which leaves plenty of room for creative displacement without damaging superficial plausibility. For example, the relevant historical documents (themselves in doubt) say the woman I used as the basis for my protagonist in *Elle* remained on the island in the Gulf of St. Lawrence for two years and some months. But I ran out of dramatic possibilities for her after a year, so I sent her back to France early. Aesthetic considerations easily trumped historical accuracy, and no one noticed.

This is also not to say that occasionally these debates about the truth or historical accuracy of novels don't sometimes erupt into frenzied public acrimony. These debates are irrelevant or relevant in a very interesting way. A case in point is the hysteria over Dan Brown's *The Da Vinci Code*. When the movie version of the novel was released, the *Toronto Star* ran a meta-commentary on the "flurry of analysis about the truth of the novel." Among other debate armatures, the *Star* mentioned the Archbishop of Canterbury's denunciation of the "lies" in the novel which might, he thought, lead Christians to doubt their faith.

One of the narrative premises on which the plot of *The Da Vinci Code* is based is the claim that Jesus was married and had a child and that child had descendants and so on and so on. This apparently contradicts the story in the Gospels which do not mention a wife or a child. We're in Salman Rushdie territory here; *The Da Vinci Code* is a novelistic attack on the roots of Christianity. But no one in Europe or North America is going to issue a fatwa against Brown because, of course, we all know a novel is a novel and not a claim on truth. At bottom, we (except for fundamentalists and people who watch too much TV) all know that a novel is already a "lie" completely imagined for our entertainment.

In fact, aside from a few small points of historical correspondence, the plausibility of a fictional text depends far more on coherence, repetition and a narrative consciousness that is always reminding us where we have been than it does on a relationship to facts. The credibility of a fictional world is built up by making the world of the text trustworthy in itself, by using consistency, reminder and repetition to create a stability of reference. In life and history, stability of reference is created by so-called facts, evidence and by the organizational categories of time and space; in novels, stability of reference is created by the repetition of characters, situations and words. And, of course, on the experimental wing of literature, there are authors who deliberately set out to subvert verisimilitude as a strategy meant to draw attention to the textuality of texts. There are examples of this type of subversion—by the use of deliberate anachronism—in both my historical novels. For example, in *The Life and Times of Captain N.*, set in the 1780s in what would later be upstate New York and Ontario, a character looks down onto a valley and says, "Someday there will be an interstate highway here." All texts are simultaneous, this line reminds us, whereas history is sequential.

The novel's reliance on repetition and internal memory or self-referentiality in its construction of fictional "truth" leads to a further observation on the difference between novels and history. Novels posit a narrative consciousness which functions as the organizing device of the whole structure. A character consciousness, whether an omniscient fictional author persona or a character or characters in the book, tells the story and remembers the book, so to speak, for the reader, using techniques which I call substitute memory devices: repetition and rehearsal (summary), tie-back lines, and character thought including memory. These substitute memory devices remind the reader of what has gone before; that is, they provide the referential stability required for the reader to enter and find his way comfortably in the world of the book.

In history, written history, there is nothing analogous to this invented character consciousness. The historian (author) stands outside the text. And he makes very little attempt, if any, inside the text, to imagine the thoughts and memories of individuals except insofar as these can be quoted or legitimately deduced from evidence. Nor do personal thoughts and memories form part of the structural foundation of the text as they do in novels. Historians may occasionally use personal thoughts and memories as evidence, and they may hypothesize motives and states of mind in order to explain events, but in a novel character consciousness is basic to the structure and not hypothetical in the least.

If a novel can sometimes be questioned in a qualified way in terms of its historical accuracy, it is equally true that at times an historical explanation can be tested by non-evidentiary means, by the demand for coherence and non-contradiction and also by the principle of Occam's Razor. Occam's Razor is a principle that rarely, if ever, comes into the composition of a novel; a novel is more of an obsessive-compulsive Rube Goldberg device that spends a good deal of its energy delaying its own ending. By contrast, history does grapple with the demand for coherence and non-contradiction but not only within the individual text, as in the case of novels, but over the discipline as a whole; unlike novels, history texts compete with each other for explanatory authority, a fact which insidiously subverts history's claim to truth. To put this slightly differently, because of the role imagination plays in interpreting evidence and because the historian and his historical text are also part of history, historical explanations for the same data can vary in alarming ways. When this happens historians can only raise their voices and shout at each other or go back to the evidence. But they will feel suddenly edgy, for the debate over interpretation raises the horrifying possibility that history itself is fiction, that history is just a novel with too many characters.

On the outlaw fringe, where all things are cast into doubt in neat antinomies, there are even theorists who might throw out evidence, the evidentiary claims of history, on the grounds that reality itself is a fiction mediated by the imagination. Kant, for example, much like Plato, divided the cosmos into the noumenal or real world and the phenomenal world or world of existence (phenomena are mediated by our perceptual apparatus and the imagination and thus, to some extent, are fictional). The noumenal or real world is timeless and unknowable and thus, on two counts, outside history. The contemporary variant of this argument has it that the day-to-day world of human existence is rendered fictional by virtue of its being mediated not only by the imagination but by the symbolic order of language itself. The question then becomes: if knowledge is always mediated, what does the unmediated world (or an historical fact) really look like? In contrast, no critic has ever meaningfully challenged the existence of novels by saying they are about something that is not real.

Imagination, Memory, Books, and History

Kant talks about the role of the imagination in cognition in *The Critique of Pure Reason* where he postulates the need, in knowing, for a third thing that mediates between raw data of perception and the mind that knows, some device for helping us recognize what we perceive. He called these templates "schema" and said they were produced by the imagination. We see a dog, he suggests, but we can't tell it's a dog until the imagination holds up a template of a dog for us to compare with the dog we are seeing. In this way, the imagination stands at the centre of all knowledge; all knowledge is a form of recognition.

The evolutionary psychologist Merlin Donald has gone much further than Kant in developing a complex of inner "faculties" required for cognition. In his book *The Origins of the Modern Mind* he suggests that humans have gone through a series of evolutionary stages involving the development of various short and long term memory faculties, controller faculties, symbol production faculties, etc. But like Kant he is basically asking the question: what sort of mental activities have to take place for us to see the world the way we see it?

Animals, Donald suggests, have a rudimentary short-duration situational memory. Proto-humans began to differentiate themselves from their ancestors not just by developing better memories but also by developing an imaginative apparatus that would allow them to reproduce or rehearse sequences of events. Or put another way, memory itself is dependent on our ability to replay imaginatively what has happened. Next comes the ability to replay the events publicly for another and the invention of dance, mime, games, rhythm and acting. Symbol production and language follow, developments that imply even more complex elaborations of inner mental faculties for producing images, remembering sequences of images, attaching meanings and so forth. Humans begin to invent what Donald calls "external memory devices" including social rituals, jewelry, personal decoration, and finally more recognizably artistic productions which lead eventually to the invention of letters and writing. But prior to the invention of writing, religion and social structure become prime repositories of large group memories that are handed down as hermetic knowledge by specially trained individuals—priests, storytellers, shamans, healers, bards and poets.

Once we invent the technology of writing, the prime receptacle for long-term memory begins to shift out of the human brain onto the printed page. The printed page allows for the retention of vast amounts of information, and it allows humans to develop new criteria for truth. Texts can be compared with each other and with external reality. At this point history and literature begin to diverge from religious practice. Within fifty years of the arrival of writing in Greece someone begins to write down *The Iliad* and *The Odyssey*, and already the gods are beginning to recede from human contact. Time becomes linear instead of cyclical (whether based on the harvest cycle or the generational cycle or the lunar cycle, etc.). Certain authoritative social functions disappear; the ancient cohesiveness of tribal society falls away. We become alienated, nostalgic and modern at the same moment.

And yet this faculty for representing what is not present is equally adept at representing what was never present, that is, fiction. In fact, the imagination seems not to make a distinction between truth and fancy, seems quite capable of generating story after story, and seems, in fact, to enjoy generating stories. This is a jarring realization for certain types of thinkers who like to have things neatly pinned down and stable. One begins to realize that there is more referential stability in a novel than there is in a work of history. As I mentioned earlier, novels don't change while history is always being challenged and re-imagined and rewritten. The spongy, imaginative element in the practice of history is also at the root of all those constant ponderous philosophical debates about whether history is an art or a science. (But let me restrain myself from leaping into that tangential swamp.)

Time, memory, imagination, social structure, religious practice and belief, language, writing, myth, story and history thus form a tightly knit matrix of evolving feedback systems. Our consciousness of time seems utterly dependent on the evolution of an imaginative ability to represent to ourselves and others events that are not immediately present. And simultaneously, our ability to represent events imaginatively is dependent on consciousness of time—sequence, before and after, etc.—which itself is dependent on the evolution of a language capable of telling time. Imagination, memory and time consciousness were for eons solely dependent on the physical human brain for storage capacity. When the technology of writing extended our ability to represent and remember, our modern ideas of time and history became possible (as the old social forms, which depended on myths and cyclical time and institutions of oral transmission of lore, disintegrated).

Novels and history developed because of the book. They are not only linked by the role imagination plays in their production but also by the fact that they are products of a specific era and a specific technology.

Before History and Novels

Recent studies of a Brazilian tribe called the Pirahã suggest that it is a people without myth, history, and even personal or group memories that stretch further than two generations. The Pirahã also have only the most rudimentary art, cannot draw, although

they do sing and whistle. What seems crucially significant is that
their language has hardly any words for number or time, nor can
they subordinate grammatical elements within sentences. The
Pirahã language appears to be a well-preserved isolate, pro-
tected by a fierce cultural conservativism among tribal members. Anthropologists and linguists are currently debating the
implications, mostly for language, of their discovery. And, of
course, one cannot draw any conclusions from a group so rare
and little studied and, yes, contemporary. But the apparent interrelation of number, time words, time consciousness, memory
and story seems suggestive if not confirmatory at some level.
This interrelation suggests the possibility that the Pirahã might
be a cultural remnant, a throwback to the time before time,
before language, memory and stories (myths) had begun to
organize the world in a recognizably human way.

But our knowledge of the Pirahã remains hazy. There are,
apparently, no native speakers who also speak another language
and who can act as translators. Anthropologists must work out
the language by learning it more or less from scratch. And what
appear to be limitations in Pirahã may in some way mirror lacu-
nae and limitations in English. In a large degree, the Pirahã
remain opaque.

What the Pirahã are now facing, however, should be familiar
to us from our own experience of the greatest human evolutionary transformation since language acquisition, the acquisition
of writing and the book. The advent of writing abruptly set in
train the effective destruction of all prior systems of thought
and social organization and initiated the conversion of oral culture to literate culture, of myth to history, of epic to novel, of
a cyclical conception of time to a linear conception of time,
of alchemy and homeopathy to modern science. We Euro-
westerners have been suffering through this metamorphosis
for five thousand years or so. Without being quite conscious
of itself as such, our Euro-western history is in fact a history of

transition, the horrid rending of a culture from within, the internecine warfare between cultural (religious, etc.) remnants and the new and the concomitant murderous quest for purity and identity. Having, by war, genocide, forced-conversion and long-running debate, adapted ourselves more or less to the new technology of the book, the new notions of historical time and the new evidence and number-based knowledge systems, we set out at the end of the fifteenth century on an era of global exploration, expansion and conquest, finding on other continents masses of people who had not evolved culturally in the same way, many of whom had not altered from a tribal-oral culture parallel to our own before the Neolithic. Our arrival was catastrophic for them and often wildly successful for us, at least in terms of material and territorial acquisition.

But precious little has been written as history about this evolutionary leap, that is, our history as the story of a clash of technologies and cultural practices, inclusive of concepts of time and systems of representation and cognition. One of the few books, to my knowledge, to begin to elucidate this clash is Tzvetan Todorov's *The Conquest of America*. And, of course, there are also wonderful anthropological studies done in Africa by Jack Goody on the contemporary transformation of a culture from orality to literacy. But in North America we seem to have refused the option of seeing our history in this way. What we have been participating in is not just history but a clash of histories, of ways of thinking about history, and the way we write our history begins with the assumption that one way of writing history is correct. In other words, the way we write history tends to extend the military and economic conquest of North America in the fifteenth and sixteenth centuries.

Two of my novels—*The Life and Times of Captain N.* and *Elle*—are set during historical epochs not our own, the 1780s and the 1540s respectively. But they are not historical novels in the sense of romantic adventure stories or costume epics, the usual popular version of the type. They are historical novels in the sense that they are about history; that is, they are about our Euro-western conception of history and other conceptions of history that preceeded it. In a sense, they are allegories of the clash of ideas, in this case the clash of ideas about history.

In *The Life and Times of Captain N.*, the forces of the new American republic represent the political philosophy derived from notions of the individual and liberty that are, in turn, derived from our modern linear view of history, history seen as progress toward a messianic goal, the city on the hill, etc. Against this are arrayed various natives and disaffected whites, more or less in shock and pessimistic about what is coming. The natives (Iroquois and Mississauga) are the tail end of an oral culture about to go down before the book, with their own mythology, their own cyclical sense of time, and their own literature based on human memory and oral transmission. Most of the characters have only vague inklings of the drama they are enacting; most do not understand how different the oral and the literate worlds really are, the impossibility of translation. The protagonist says he is against the future, which means is he also against history, a Euro-western conception of history, and he says becoming an Indian is like entering a swarming madness. He doesn't understand the madness, but at least he knows the mental framework of a native is radically different from his own.

In *Elle*, I made more of an attempt to write my characters into the "swarming madness" both literally and metaphorically, that is, into the "historical" narrative of the other. Elle enacts the essential structure of contact and colonization when she unwittingly walks into Itslk's mythic bear-hunt quest and then finds herself absorbed into the oral-magical-dream world of the bear woman. This portion of the novel has been most difficult for readers to read because it amounts to an epic intrusion into the modern form of the novel. The words go on but the text twists on some barely imaginable axis. I make no claim for its correctness as a representation of how a native might have thought. I did want to make it somewhat unreadable in a way that might provoke the reader into thinking about the character of difference.

In this context, the phrase "swarming madness" and my word "unreadable" have the same notional referent. In both novels, I posit the thesis that the technological "superiority" that shocked, demoralized and ultimately defeated the natives was not just a matter of arms, gunpowder and microbes but also, and perhaps primarily, the book. We know from contemporary experience in Vietnam and Iraq and Afghanistan that mere material technological superiority does not guarantee conquest. The book defeated the oral culture of America (of course, in parts of America the oral culture was already shifting toward some sort of written word though not enough, yet, to have changed the way those people thought). And it did this by undermining a cultural system of thought (ways of deciding truth, myth, history, ritual, kinship and land-use patterns, etc.). Simply put, a book is better for retaining certain sorts of memories than the human brain. A culture which bases its knowledge on human memory and oral transmission suffers limitations in contrast to a bookish culture not only in terms of scale and quantity but also in terms of the criteria it brings to bear in order to decide what is knowledge or not. This is the point Todorov makes in his book about Cortez and the Aztecs. The Aztec leaders could not believe the factual reports of their own scouts and diplomats. It was easier to subsume the arrival of the Spaniards, uneasily, under the categories supplied by traditional—ritual and mythic—lore.

This is not to say they were simply credulous savages; it means that their highly sophisticated intellectual modes of thought were too rigid and inflexible to assimilate quickly the surprising new thing. All cultures and knowledge systems can absorb the new, if only by arguing from analogy—but only up to a point. At a certain point, the new is so alien as to be incomprehensible. If we think in terms of referential stability, that phrase I introduced earlier, we can say that in an oral culture referential stability is supplied by the authority of a traditional speaker or the priestly class, that is, in the continuity of oral transmission and an oral culture's respect for the word as such. But since oral transmission depends upon human memory, with an emphasis on rote learning, the elements of knowledge so passed on must be relatively limited and static, hence the rigidity of such a structure, with a premium placed on tradition, repetition and sameness.

In an oral culture, the social system, kinship pattern, art, mythic stories, ritual, life stages and so on become elaborate interrelated and mirroring mnemonic devices that reinforce identity. In a book culture, all the energy formerly used in remembering is suddenly freed up for other purposes such as investigating the new thing. Our culture chews through the new like termites in a woodpile simply because we don't have to remember anything anymore. In fact, the speed of our technological and scientific advance is directly relatable to the invention of larger and larger external storage devices. At the same time, the social structure itself, no longer useful to jog our memory about the way things are, loses its old cohesiveness. Theory and critical thinking become possible as we compare texts, and science and history become possible when we can compare text with evidence. And truth changes location—from the authoritative voice of the elders to the new disciplines of observation and induction.

This change in consciousness is discontinuous; it creates an abrupt rupture with the past. An oral culture takes ages to begin to learn to translate the words of a literate culture into its own language. But a literate culture can never recover the oral consciousness that it has lost. We can write things down, record ritual, folklore and epic, and read about them later, but we cannot ever recall how it felt to be a druid. This "truth" is underlined by the experience of Daniel Everett, the anthropologist chiefly involved in studying the aforementioned Pirahã. He spent seven years with the tiny tribe and knows it as well as anyone who is not a native speaker. His major paper on the Pirahã is called "Cultural Constraints on Grammar and Cognition in Pirahã" and it concludes—actually it's the last of the endnotes—with this amazing observation.

> One morning in 1980, during a nine-month stay with the Pirahã, I awoke to yelling, crying, and whooping near the river's edge, about fifty feet from where I was trying vainly to sleep. I went to the crowd, which included nearly every man, woman, and child in the village. They were all pointing across the river and some were crying, some were yelling, and all were acting as though what they were seeing was very frightening. I looked across the river, but I could see nothing. I asked them what they were fussing about. One man answered incredulously, 'Can't you see him there?' 'I see nothing. What are you talking about?' was my response. 'There, on the other side, on that small strip of beach, is **'igagaí** a mean not-blood-one.' There was nothing on the other side. But the people insisted that he was there in full view. This experience has haunted me ever since. It underscored how spirits are not merely fictional characters to the Pirahã, but concrete experiences.

Everett's confusion over the experience of Pirahã ghosts, his sense of being haunted by a world of experience that he cannot share, relegated to an endnote, somehow draws into question the certainty of the entire modern project. In this encounter, basic ideas such as experience, fact, truth and evidence begin to shift suddenly and alarmingly (no wonder he shoved it into an endnote). His paper is about translation, about the difficulty of penetrating the other's mind; but at the end he is vouchsafed an experience of otherness so alien as to be irremediably outside his ability even to sense what others around him are sensing. So that the title of his essay—"Cultural Constraints on Grammar and Cognition in Pirahã"—could justifiably be inverted to read "Cultural Constraints on Grammar and Cognition *in English*." Though, of course, Everett does not see it that way and remains only "haunted" and perhaps ever so vaguely nostalgic—the modern mood.

After History, a Prologue

In North America, Africa, Polynesia, Australia, etc., we Euro-westerners have stood by as if mesmerized, watching ourselves and our destruction of oral cultures as if from the outside (the vantage point of history). For the most part we have not engaged in their experience of this destruction except in the tired old tragic categories of massacre, injustice, plague and technological superiority. In no more than four or five centuries we have demanded of these cultures that they grow up, assimilate and become like us—forgetting our own 5,000 or so years of adjustment yet to be completed. We have written their history mostly as our history, a history of conquest or guilt.

In the latter half of the twentieth century there has been some lip service paid to the notion of native history. This is an interesting point to meditate upon. In practice, this means an accommodation by which historians have seen fit to allow native oral lore as corroborative evidence for some historical events. Thus Mississauga oral reports of a migration south into southwestern Ontario in the late seventeenth century and a subsequent skirmishing war with the upstate New York Iroquois, especially the Seneca, have generally been credited as true. But, though I accept that these efforts are well meant, there is something logically opaque about the reasoning. Historians ask themselves, What would native history look like? and answer the question by examining oral reports (ironically, these reports are written down as soon as possible). But these oral reports are not "history." What would native history look like? is the wrong question. Calling oral traditions "history" or even "proto-history" is an old way of thinking, thinking by analogy. Something like: What is the closest thing natives do that looks like history? We'll call it history and make the natives look more modern than they are.

But the argument is a kind of backwards assimilation, an effort to include native reports by denying their difference. Native oral reports are not as specific or concrete as history, nor are they warranted by an appeal to evidence or calibrated against an objective time scale. (What makes the Maya hiero-glyphs slightly closer to real history is the fact that they are cali-brated against a calendar, and, of course, they are written down. Somehow the two go together—the modern obsession with information storage and time keeping.) Their authority, their "truth" (a third kind of truth, truth by authority and custom—as opposed to truth by evidence or truth by coherence) resides in memory and their mode of transmission. In fact, as history, they have only a limited suggestive value.

In the same way, the invention of the book changed literary form. Epic literature, the oral mode, depends on repetition, mnemonic epithets (instead of characterization), the recycling of conventional motifs and the memory and inspiration of the individual performer. Often, when these performances are writ-ten down, they seem thin, trite, repetitious and moralizing to the modern reader. This isn't an issue of quality of work or aes-thetics or taste; it's an issue of different kinds of literary produc-tion and differently trained readers. Written down, the stories of an oral culture do not "mean" in the way they meant in the time before books. And the narrative consciousness deployed as a structural principle in novels and short stories is radically unlike that in a folktale. In his essay "The Storyteller" Walter

Benjamin wrote, "The earliest symptom of a process whose end is the decline of storytelling is the rise of the novel at the beginning of modern times." In this regard, novels and history are much closer to each other, much more alike, in contrast to the oral productions of an earlier time.

Everett, writing about that haunting experience by the river in Brazil, betrays something of our basic cultural assumptions when he uses the phrase "fictional characters" in contrast to the phrase "concrete experiences." To us, everything that is not a concrete experience is fictional, that is, we divide experience, funneled, as I've said, through the imagination, as either history or novel. To put this another way, in our culture, we tend to deny the fictional nature, that is, the imaginative component, of so-called concrete experience. In our culture, the epic has given way to the novel, history has replaced myth, and science has replaced astrology, homeopathy, ritual healing and alchemy. We can no longer even imagine the inner quality of a mind or a culture in which these are legitimate intellectual activities. Nor can we, apparently, imagine what it is like to live within a culture whose every mode of constructing truth is systematically cast into doubt and delegitimized. We are used to describing the destruction of native culture in ritualized ways: we disrupted their land-use patterns, their traditional hunting and fishing patterns; we enslaved them, massacred them and infected them with deadly diseases. We explain rampant alcoholism on reserves by saying such things, and the natives themselves say it, grasping at straws, using bits and pieces of ready-made language to explain the inexplicable.

What has been missed in all this debate of traditionalism vs. assimilation, conquest vs. vanquished, is an historical consciousness that addresses the process of transformation the natives are undergoing and all that entails in terms of social disintegration and personal alienation. And of course the responsibility for this lacuna lies not only with the Euro-western conquering race but with the natives themselves. An example of native efforts in this regard exists in the feature movie *The Journals of Knud Rasmussen,* directed by the filmmakers Zacharias Kunuk and Norman Cohn (who also made *Atanarjuat, The Fast Runner*). Written and filmed by Inuit, the movie is based on early 20th century Danish ethnographic studies—notice the inter-cultural message loop—and focuses on the character of a shaman struggling to choose between adopting Christianity or following his traditional way of life.

What makes this transformation itself all the more uncertain and ambiguous is that the so-called literate culture of conquest is itself also in a state of transition—into what we cannot tell. Call it postmodern or the information age, it amounts to the same inscrutable future. The advent of computer storage and retrieval systems and networked human relations (separate from family, local community, city or country) promises, one would guess, to have an evolutionary impact somewhat akin to that of writing and the book, only more so. Thus around the world remnants of oral cultures are being asked to transform themselves into that which already can no longer name itself. This is fascinating and should be watched. We should be watching ourselves as we watch them and wondering what comes after history and novels.

DON QUIXOTE, ROSEMARY'S BABY, ALIEN, AND THE FRENCH LIEUTENANT'S WOMAN

MEDITATIONS ON THE IDEOLOGY OF CLOSURE AND THE COMFORTING LIE

I wish now to speak of endings, which are something people don't often talk about because they come, well, at the end, and sometimes by the end of a book or a story we're not paying all that much attention except to the way the plot turns out. When I was writing my book on *Don Quixote*, I noticed that other books about *Don Quixote* took many or most of their examples from the first half of the novel, as though their authors had gotten impatient and inattentive as they rushed to the end (the oft-cited windmills, for example, appear in Chapter 8). To remedy this, as I was writing my book, I was also rereading the novel backwards one chapter at a time so that I could give lots of examples from the closing bits.

But then I noticed how some critics found the end of *Don Quixote* troubling and problematic for reasons I will go into shortly, and that reminded me of how I find most endings problematic, which in turn raises all sorts of interesting questions about the artificiality of form in contrast with the common sense aesthetic ideal of verisimilitude. It's a truism that life doesn't come in neat boxes but art does. To be sure, life does come in a kind of box as well, birth and death (and, after that, a nice pine box). But birth and death are absolutes in a way that the ends of stories are not. We come to the end of life, the wall, as it were, of our little box and then, pffft!—nothing. This renders stories peculiarly comforting; the end of a story is like a death, but then you think, hey, here I am, still alive, ready to pick up another book and start again.

So what do *Don Quixote, Rosemary's Baby, Alien* and *The French Lieutenant's Woman* have in common? Well, they are all stories of a sort and all have endings, and when you look at them cumulatively they begin to speak to each other in fascinating and instructive ways. You may remember that John Fowles' novel has two endings, one a conventional marriage ending and the other a more modern feminist ending with the female lead going off to be an independent operator leaving the hero in her dust. At the end of *Rosemary's Baby*, Rosemary decides to be a mother to the son of Satan, embracing the evil that has been stalking her throughout the movie. And at the end of *Alien*, Ripley, played by Sigourney Weaver, flushes the monster out the shuttle's rocket engine (the mother ship is called the Nostromo—so perhaps someone was thinking of Conrad there), though we just know we haven't heard the end of him or her yet, leaving open the possibility of a sequel (and, in the sequels, Ripley tries to flush the monster again and then gives birth to a baby monster while throwing herself and the baby into a vat of molten lead only to be reborn as a hybrid human-monster clone in the—so far—last of the series in which she kills the beast again and returns to earth with her android buddy—also a hybrid creature). Which leads us to *Don Quixote* the second half of which is already a sequel to the first half (published ten years apart—it's fascinating to notice that near the end of the second half Cervantes began to sew in the bridge to yet another sequel, one in which Quixote buys a flock of sheep and becomes a romantic, poetry-spouting shepherd). But when *Don Quixote* finally does come to a stop, it ends on a note so unsatisfactory that it has mystified some scholars and not a few readers ever since; that is, the old knight (he's not so old really, just fifty, but we tend to think of him as old) simply goes home, gets into bed, announces that he is sane again (having been a victim of a comic violent lunacy for 800 pages) and dies. (You can read *Quixote* as *Alien* written from the point of view of the monster; Quixote himself is the monster and the student, Samson Carrasco, is Ripley.)

The ending of *Don Quixote* is often deemed unsatisfactory, as I said, for a couple of reasons: first of all, there's no explanation for Quixote's change of heart, no motivation; and, second, and this is especially wounding to those who identify with the sentimental or romantic dream-the-impossible-dream interpretation of the novel, the ending denies the idealistic premise on which the novel seems to operate, that is, that it's a good thing to follow one's dreams and aspire to high ideals. Don Quixote is adamantly against dreams and high ideals on his deathbed; he's certain all that stuff he used to believe about Dulcinea and knights errant is pure insanity. And he's right. That's the way the novel is written. At the outset, Alonso Quixano is driven insane by reading adventure romance novels in the medieval mode, and at the end he returns to sanity and reality. But it's such a humdrum reality that even Quixote's friends—the curate, the barber, the student and Sancho Panza—cannot bear to see the old man recant his fevered dreams. They realize at once that realism is death (they realize Quixote will die) and they also suspect that Quixote's refound realism, his common sense and sensibility, are just another form of insanity. They spend the last few pages of the novel trying to reignite in Alonso the Good his former violent fancies that sent him out on adventures, regretting, as all good readers at the end of a book, the end of the entertainment and the death of their beloved friend.

"Ah!" said Sancho weeping, "don't die, master, but take my advice and live many years; for the foolishest thing a man can do in this life is to let himself die without rhyme or reason, without anybody killing him, or any hands but melancholy's making an end of him. Come, don't be lazy, but get up from your bed and let us take to the fields in shepherd's trim as we agreed. Perhaps behind some bush we shall find the lady Dulcinea disenchanted, as fine as fine can be. If it be that you are dying of vexation at having been vanquished, lay the blame on me, and say you were overthrown because I had girthed Rocinante badly; besides you must have seen in your books of chivalry that it is a common thing for knights to upset one another, and for him who is conquered to-day to be conqueror tomorrow."

Abstract some patterns. I am always looking for new metaphors for describing what is going on in a story or a novel or a movie for that matter. In every one of the works in hand the story itself posits a ground, a situation, a position of what, for want of a better word, we'll call normality. In *Rosemary's Baby* a nice young couple is looking for a cheap but larger apartment. In *Alien* a commercial spaceship is towing a crippled freighter back to port. The crew wakes up from a space nap griping about shares, wages and food. In *The French Lieutenant's Woman* the Victorian fossil hound, Charles, is about to be married to a rich merchant's daughter and embark on a life of conventional ease and scientific eccentricity. And in *Don Quixote* Alonso Quixano is fifty, likes to hunt, reads books, has probably never had sex (suffers from what Tobias Smollett translates as "imbecility of the loins"), lives with his housekeeper and his niece and has had a twelve-year crush on a girl in the village to whom he cannot even bring himself to speak.

In each story, we are saved from this non-story-ish, humdrum normality by the eruption of something abnormal. In *Quixote*, the old don goes insane from reading books in the first couple of pages of the novel and embarks on the first of his adventures. In *Rosemary's Baby* an ironically ordinary-looking coven of Satan-worshippers manipulates Rosemary into a fantastically public and yet bestial rape, the closest we ever come to actually seeing the evil that lurks. In *Alien* the "company" sends Ripley's crew unwittingly to retrieve a horribly perfect killing monster—the alien creature of the title. (As I said earlier, I like the way these works start talking to each other right away. The *Alien* movies and *Rosemary's Baby* are so much about motherhood and pregnancy—in *Alien* the curious Kane gets the Rosemary role and gives birth on the dining room table of the Nostromo through his chest. In the sequel we meet the mother alien, and never has anything so fantastically ugly looked quite so sympathetic. In the third movie, Ripley herself gives birth—through the chest—just as she lets herself fall into the molten lead, and we catch glimpses of her, Rosemary-like, cuddling her monstrous baby in the seconds before they die.) And in *The French Lieutenant's Woman* the plot swings into action when Charles simply sees Sarah Woodruff standing alone at the end of the mole—one conventional plot has always turned on the quaint idea that a single woman, outside the socially-sanctioned tether of marriage, is a monster of outlaw desire on the loose. (Hence both *Quixote* and *The French Lieutenant's Woman* begin with a shy bookish guy seeing a woman from afar and stamping her with a romantic libidinal fancy that is presented as a kind of madness or an idea that leads to broken marriage vows and social disgrace.)

To abstract the pattern a little further, each of these works is about a discourse of normality, of social tranquility, smashed by the eruption of an alien force (actual aliens or single women who arouse alien thoughts; I will not dwell here on what it is about western culture—and, of course, it's not just western culture—that seems to want to group monstrous aliens and single women under the same heading of threat). This makes me think of the psychoanalyst Jacques Lacan and his concepts of the Symbolic and the Real, which are his versions of the metaphysical dualism that has haunted Western philosophy since Plato. The Symbolic is the linguistic voice of authority, normality and reality, as it were, the net of words into which we fit ourselves in order to call ourselves our selves and our world the world in the first place. The Real is whatever exists, if it exists, beyond the definitions of the Symbolic—no doubt I am grossly over-simplifying for the purpose of being, well, simple. Whatever it is, the Real is beyond, and it only impinges on us in an accidental and generally horrific way—death or some physical cataclysm. But the Real is also what is repressed, the thing that doesn't fit in the realm of the net of words we call the Symbolic. Or it is the surplus of meaning or stain which prevents us from fitting into the net.

This idea of the net of words which veils or papers over the thing-that-is-beyond sheds other concepts. The act of repression is itself some hint of a Real that is kept mostly under wraps. Then there is the concept of the return of the repressed; that is, the sense in which the repressed Real insists on being present to us even if its presence is only notable in the effort it takes us to keep ignoring it (it insists, one supposes, because it's there whereas everything else that we think of as real in the ordinary sense isn't quite there in the same way). Symptoms are acting out behav-

iours we deploy to cover up instances of the insistence of the
Real; symptoms are signs of the presence nearby of the Real
though they are fictional constructs in themselves. This leads
to some strange logical reversals. In a sense, what we see as normally real is a fiction, the product of repression. Normal life
isn't life at all. And symptoms become manifestations of something other than the fiction of normal life insisting on being
recognized.

You get a kind of neo-romantic riff going with this: humdrum reality is actually an illness and things we normally think
of as illness are perhaps hints of something more healthy going
on. In *Don Quixote*, the old knight's friends set out to cure him of
his mania, but their cure doesn't involve going up to him and
trying to convince him that the way he sees the world is mis-
guided (a conventional therapeutic cure). Instead, they enter
into his mania, dress up in disguise, and devise elaborate conspir-
acies in order to trick him into going home and abandoning his
crazy lifestyle. In the second half of the novel, the student, Samson Carrasco, dresses up like a knight-errant and goes chasing
after Quixote in order to fight battles with him, going "insane"
himself, as his pretend-squire tells Sancho, that another man
might become sane. The first time he fights Quixote he loses,
but the second time he wins—that fateful encounter on the
beach at Barcelona—and forces Quixote to swear to leave off
knight-errantry for the period of two years. At the end of the
novel, the curate, the barber, Samson and Sancho, realizing, like
all good readers, that the life of fiction is more interesting than
the death-in-life of humdrum reality, strive to reignite Quixote's
mania using his own old arguments which they once abhorred.
Among other things, *Don Quixote* is a novel about the experience of reading a novel, and the end of the book is an allegory
of the disappointment we all feel when we reach, yes, the end of
a book.

In *The French Lieutenant's Woman* John Fowles offers us two endings, as I say, explicitly recognizing, just as Cervantes does, the bookish nature of books (this is a kind of aesthetic hyper-realism). One ending is the conventional marriage ending, the celebration of love and family values we have come to expect as standard romance fare, this kind of romance being the descendent of ancient, pre-literate spring fertility rituals. Jane Austen's novels end with marriages—even if, as in *Mansfield Park*, for example, the marriage seems somewhat forced on the heroine who has, possibly, earned the love of a better man. In this novelistic universe, the eruption of the Real—read, in this instance, uncontrolled sexual desire—is subdued to the discourse of social order. Fowles' other ending presents Sarah, as I say, as an independent operator, a modern emancipated woman who refuses the role of Symbol of the Real and Object of Male Desire and tells Charles to go away and let her get on with her own life. Charles either gets the girl in the end and by marriage turns the inappropriate object of his affections into an appropriate object, or he's abandoned by the female and becomes an existential hero, whether he likes it or not. Fowles is saying, of course, that the socially sanctioned novel-ending—marriage—is a fictional construct, part of the Symbolic. He is offering a critique of conventional eighteenth and nineteenth century novels just as Cervantes was offering a tongue-in-cheek critique of the medieval romances that drove Quixote mad. He is telling us, ever so delicately, that some endings can play into the hands of the keepers of social order, that novels themselves can support the Symbolic and participate in the repression of the Real. And, of course, we have to ask ourselves if that's what we want our novels and stories to do.

If we look at *Alien* and *Rosemary's Baby*, we find a similarly instructive pairing. In *Alien* Ripley becomes the Western hero, the Gary Cooper loner who single-handedly flushes evil (the

Real, perfect killing machine, unappeasable desire for destruction) out of the system. At the end of the movie, she goes to
sleep with Jones the cat, assured that everything is back to normal. It's only the lingering camera that hints to the viewer that
something else is watching, that a sequel is in the making (odd
to think that the movie viewer and the lingering evil coincide in
the gaze—what do we make of that?). In *Rosemary's Baby*, however, normality is subverted ironically in that moment when
Rosemary overcomes her fear and disgust (what does that baby
look like?) and allows her motherly instincts to overcome her
yearning for goodness and normality. This is a curious and disturbing ending because the heroine (think what Ripley does
with her evil baby) acquiesces to evil, joins the fantasmal company of the repressed. One of the things convention fears the
most is that there might be good reasons for turning bad (and,
of course, it's a woman who finds the way).

Ripley is the conventional storybook heroine here, the
character who spends her energy sewing up the tear in the discourse of normal reality. Rosemary abandons or at least distorts
the discourse of reality for her own ends which happen to coincide with the ends of evil. She'll bring up Satan's child even if
he does have funny ears. Because we are who we are (children of
the Lacanian Symbolic) we are trained to find Ripley's ending
morally and emotionally satisfying in a way none of the other
endings I've been talking about can achieve. We are trained to
expect marriages at the end of romance stories and expulsion
at the end of alien monster stories (there are two ways of dealing
with aliens—absorb them into the self, say, by marrying them,
or expel them). In contrast, the ending of *Don Quixote* seems
slightly unsatisfying because Quixote never quite recognizes
the threat of his own mania and doesn't really struggle to right
himself. His enemies are all imagined as is the woman he claims
to love. He just decides to embrace the normal at the end of the

book while his friends urge him to go crazy again. The struggle to be good guarantees the heft of the outcome—simply deciding to be good, read ironically, might mean that there's no difference between being good or being crazy; both alternatives might be equally fictional.

The French Lieutenant's Woman offers two endings with divergent moral outcomes. We can ask ourselves in hindsight if the independent female ending is really all that divergent, if it doesn't simply play into a variant of the Symbolic, a message loop that puts more of a premium on female labour than biological reproduction. But perhaps that is less important than Fowles' realization that the ending of a novel carries a tacit or not so tacit moral, and this ending is often culturally normative. *Rosemary's Baby* ends with a cheeky subversion of the conventional ending which we get in spades in *Alien*. Ripley is the ancient hero-prince-knight who combats the monster of the Real to ensure the quiet, prudent, productive lives of normal people. The struggle is brutal, the ending is clean (except for the sequel thing). Actually, *Alien* is very much a modern version of those medieval historical romances which drive Quixote mad at the beginning of his novel. This is fascinating because it suggests that Cervantes, so early in the development of the novel as a form, already understood the social-moral function of conventional plots and endings. He knew that a truly superlative novel had to play against convention in some way in order, as it were, to clarify the nature of convention itself, that he had to write a book against books. *Don Quixote* is a book about what Alain Badiou has called our "passion for the real" which yet recognizes the essentially fictional nature of all realities. His plot is pure symptom since there never is a real enemy in the book. *Alien* is satisfying in a certain level because we long for the Real to show itself, to come out and do battle. We wouldn't have much chance against it, that's true. But some plucky big-haired girl might come along . . .

As I reach here for closure myself, two other famous literary endings come to mind. At the end of *War and Peace* Tolstoy inserts an extended essay on the nature of history. We also find out that instead of living happily ever after (there's a marriage-ending at the end of the conventional novel text), Pierre and Natasha end up living obscurely thwarted and confusing bourgeois lives, Pierre drifting into political intrigue and freemasonry at the end of the end. Tolstoy subverts the conventional ending with irony and mixed form (that essay). In contrast, he preserves the moralizing tone of *Anna Karenina* to the end— Levin has a good marriage; Anna, the free radical, the feminine semblance of the Real, kills herself (in order to repress the thing that she reminds everyone of). At the end of "Heart of Darkness" Conrad does something equally odd: Marlow goes to Africa, finds Kurtz, and nearly dies himself. He has descended into Hell (the Real) and consorted with a hero of the Dark Side. But at the end of the story he goes to Brussels to look up Kurtz's intended wife and when he finds her, rather than tell her the truth, he lies and says that her name was on Kurtz's lips when he died. His reason for doing this is that it would be too awful for her to know the truth, that women and other generally normal people (yes, yes, besides being outlaws of desire, women are also symbolized as the opposite—dutiful, normal, stay-at-homes) need conventional lies to support their version of reality, that, in fact, what we think of as normal society couldn't function without the comforting conventional lie. With his lie, Conrad/Marlow/Ripley delivers the message of the Symbolic and, for the intended, sews up the tattered discourse of normal reality. He keeps her necessary illusions intact.

(It's fascinating how often the idea of a guardian figure pops up in literature since it was first invented in Plato's *Republic*; by guardian figure, I mean the one who, wiser and braver than the rest, approaches and does battle with the Real in order to preserve the innocent, fictional harmony of the normal while himself receiving obscure wounds that never heal—think: the Fisher King of the Grail legends. Ripley is a version of the hero-guardian whereas Rosemary betrays the normal—and, in any case, in the ironic world of that movie there is nothing more irritatingly normal than the witches who manipulate her. Marlow is a guardian, but Quixote, who fancies himself a guardian, never amounts to one because of the totally fictional nature of the universe he inhabits—he can't find anything real to battle against and most people need protection from him. Cervantes' multiple ironies mock Plato at every turn.)

This brings us to an interesting distinction between stories that preserve our illusions of a conventional reality and those that deny the reality of the real. This is not, I hasten to add, a distinction between different versions of what is real. The novels of Socialist Realism were often Tolstoyan in scope and technique but like many run-of-the-mill modern novels were written inside a particular system of belief about the nature of reality (and the debates allowed within that system—the illusion of freedom). The Tolstoy of *War and Peace*, much like Cervantes, knew how much we want things to be real while being thwarted at every ironic turn by the totally fictional nature of what is. I am reminded here of one of my literary touchstones: in Alice Munro's story "Meneseteung," the spinster poetess Almeda Roth gets stoned on nerve medicine and sees flowers and tombstones walking down the street of her nineteenth century Ontario village. And I quote:

> No need for alarm.
> For she hasn't thought that crocheted roses could float away or that tombstones could hurry down the street. She doesn't mistake that for reality, and neither does she mistake anything else for reality, and that is how she knows that she is sane.

There has long been a debate in North America over the moral function of fiction. It has always seemed a bit beside the point to me, one of those allowable debates that never draws into question the context of the debate itself, that is, never calls into question the nature of moral behaviour or the nature of reality presupposed in the debate. Another way of looking at this is to ask who gives permission for the debate to go forward, who sets the questions, and what sort of debate, in contrast, would not be allowed?

The *Alien* movies seem quite brilliant to me in their way, viscerally satisfying because we have been so well-trained to believe in clear distinctions between self and other (alien), of pollution and purity. So knowing are these movies that they play little games within the conceptual framework, introducing androids (bad at the beginning and getting better as the series wears on), which are like us but not us, and criminals as aliens within (that prison in the third movie), the monster baby Ripley almost seems to love, and hybrid Ripleys (that amazing scene in the lab in the fourth movie with all the various failed clone versions of Ripley in glass tanks). But the emphasis on fine gradations of purity is straight out of the Old Testament, and the films' persistent anti-science bias (a knee-jerk bias that bespeaks the fundamentally anti-intellectual, if not to say simply simple-minded, premise of the films—talk about your allowable debates—think here: intelligent design, and ask yourselves what debate is being deflected into the allowable debate over intelligent design).

Stories are traditionally the bearers of, well, tradition. The ancient stories we remember as a culture were meant to teach us how the culture itself works. Form isn't automatically value free. The very fact that a story is a neat package implies the somewhat doubtful premise that the world comes to us in neat packages. Endings themselves carry a tacit metaphysical assumption which we might, in fact, want to call into question. The Russian critic

Mikhail Bakhtin has made popular the romantic notion that novels, as a form (in contrast to the form of epics), are subversive. And I think we tend to take for granted that when we write novels and stories we are doing something vaguely adventurous and new. But the truth is that many novels and stories simply and unthinkingly endorse the social and cultural values within which they are written. These can be very entertaining works, brilliant, as I say, in their own right. Often, within a culture, a novel can in fact even extend the envelope of allowable debate. Dickens' novels, for example, contributed to the debate on child labour in Victorian England and lampooned a rickety, criminally complex justice system. But time and time again the most popular works in a culture are those that most skillfully suggest our worst fears and yet offer reassurance at the end with appropriate closure. Watch the endings. It doesn't matter how direct and harshly realistic the middle content of a work is; the ending can gloss it over. This is what Conrad's peculiar ending means—I, the author, can tell you a grim story about the heart of darkness and the illimitable corruptibility of the human soul, and I can tell you a comforting lie at the end (in this case, Kurtz's fiancée stands in for the reader). In other words, even quite challenging stories can be rescinded by a clever ending. And most stories are, in the end (pun intended), little more than bedtime stories for children.

But Conrad's ending, like Cervantes' in its own off-handedly ironic way, like Fowles' double ending, and like Rosemary's turn to the dark side, points in a different direction. (Think here, by the way, of Laurence Sterne's *Tristram Shandy*, a great novel about, among other things, never being able to come to the end of the novel.) We want to ask ourselves what a story without an ending might look like? What is the nature and form of a non-ending or an ending that draws into question the idea of endings? As always we must look at literature itself for suggestive examples. I've given you a few to think about, but there are many more. Looking for them is a little like birdwatching, you have to sneak around in the underbrush and keep your eyes open. And, above all, we must become aware of our own formal assumptions when writing and begin to question even our apparently instinctive and most visceral reactions to endings.

That Alice Munro story I mentioned is a case in point. The story shifts back and forth between the deeply interior third person in the mind of the spinster poet Almeda Roth and a corporate community point of view anchored to quotations from the local newspaper, *The Vidette*. In Almeda's head we get that wonderful passage I cited earlier about reality and sanity, but Munro cagily gives the last word to the community voice, literally the voice of Lacan's Symbolic, and that voice judges Almeda harshly for being a woman and a spinster and a poet. To her village, Almeda became a dotty old lady. This point of view shift illustrates the power of that corporate voice against anyone who is different, any individual. Munro knows who gets the last word. But the story delivers traditional closure with a wise and ever so slightly comic irony that undercuts its own ending.

What, then, is the story of this so-called Real with a capital r? My guess is that it won't be anything we recognize. This is how Conrad, with the slyest of ironies, describes it in "Heart of Darkness":

"No, it is impossible; it is impossible to convey the life-sensation of any given epoch of one's existence—that which makes its truth, its meaning—its subtle and penetrating essence. It is impossible. We live, as we dream—alone."

He paused again as if reflecting, then added:

"Of course in this you fellows see more than I could then. You see me, who you know. . . ."

It had become so pitch dark that we listeners could hardly see one another. For a long time already he, sitting apart, had been no more to us than a voice. There was not a word from anybody. The others might have been asleep, but I was awake. I listened, I listened on the watch for the sentence, for the word, that would give me the clue to the faint uneasiness inspired by this narrative that seemed to shape itself without human lips in the heavy night-air of the river.

ACKNOWLEDGMENTS

"How to Write a Novel" was originally published as "Notes on Novel Structure" in "Douglas Glover: A Short Course in Narrative Structure" in *The New Quarterly*, Number 87, Summer 2003. A somewhat rewritten version was published in *Words Overflown by Stars, Creative Writing Instruction and Insight from the Vermont College of Fine Arts MFA Program*, edited by David Jauss, Writers Digest Books, Cincinnati, 2009.

"How to Write a Short Story: Notes on Structure and an Exercise" was originally published in "Douglas Glover: A Short Course in Narrative Structure" in *The New Quarterly*, Number 87, Summer 2003.

"Attack of the Copula Spiders: Thoughts on Writing Well in a Post-Literate Age" appeared in *The New Quarterly*, Number 103, Summer, 2007.

"The Drama of Grammar" appeared in *The New Quarterly*, Number 105, Winter 2008. It won the magazine's 2008 Edna Award for Non-Fiction.

"The Mind of Alice Munro" appeared in a special short story issue of *Canadian Notes & Queries*, Summer, 2010.

"How to Read a Mark Anthony Jarman Short Story" appeared in *Wild Writers We Have Known: A Celebration of the Canadian Short Story and Story Writers, A Special Double Issue of The New Quarterly*, V. XXI, Numbers 2 & 3, Summer/Fall 2001.

"Novels and Dreams: On Leon Rooke's *A Good Baby*" appeared in *White Gloves of the Doorman, The Works of Leon Rooke*, Edited by Branko Gorjup, Exile Editions, Toronto, 2004.

"Before/After History and the Novel" began life as a lecture at the L. R. Wilson Centre in Canadian History at McMaster University. In this rewritten form, it appeared in *upstreet*, Number 6, 2010.

"*Don Quixote, Rosemary's Baby, Alien,* and *The French Lieutenant's Woman*: Meditations on the Ideology of Closure and the Comforting Lie" appeared in *upstreet*, Number 4, 2008.